The Romance and Poems of
EDGAR ALLAN POE
&
SARAH
HELEN
WHITMAN

Fourth Edition, Expanded & Revised

With an essay
by Brett Rutherford

Illustrations
by Richard Sardinha

LAST

FLOWERS

The Poet's Press

PITTSBURGH, PA

Fourth edition, 2011
Second printing, 2016
This is the 195th publication of
THE POET'S PRESS
2209 Murray Avenue #3/ Pittsburgh PA 15217
www.poetspress.org

ISBN 0922558-60-4
Also published as an e-book
in Adobe Acrobat.

CONTENTS

POE & MRS. WHITMAN:
RAVEN AND DOVE

Anyone who has ever thrilled to the euphony and cadences of Poe — either as a youngster, or, like myself, as a super-annuated youth — has no doubt wondered: were there *others* like Poe? Was he unique in his cosmic scope, his brooding and fevered flight into worlds of fantasy, his nocturnal haunting of tombs and cypress groves? There *was* at least one other — the Providence poet Sarah Helen Whitman. This brilliant and eccentric woman was Poe's spiritual equal, and their calamitous romance was one of the great misfortunes in the history of literature. Their poetry, published here together for the first time, demonstrates not only the depth of her intellect, but the remarkable ways in which their works complement one another.

In this book you will encounter a poet whose mind encompasses the entire range of 19th Century Romanticism, and whose poems, under the spell of Poe, walk side by side with his in the misty mid-regions of Weir.

Is she Poe's literary equal? Alas, there is only one Poe. But as a companion and sequel to Poe, she has much to recommend her. If you love Poe, you will like or even love Sarah Helen Whitman. If your heart is open to the passion, sorrow and tragedy of this "almost" liaison of two brilliant intellects, you will find this colloquy of their poems a wrenching one.

The Powers in Rhode Island:
A Brief Chronology

Edgar Allan Poe visited Providence, Rhode Island six times, beginning in September 1848, to win the affections and promise of marriage of Sarah Helen Whitman. He spent as many as 28 days in the College Hill neighborhood, an area still haunted today by memories of his presence. Grief-stricken after the death of his young wife Virginia by consumption, and

<9>

alienated from the New York *literati,* Poe conducted an intense but doomed courtship of Rhode Island's most prominent female poet. She would live until 1878, publishing her poetry and fostering generations of younger writers and artists; Poe, hurtling to his ruin, had less than ten months to live when he left Providence for the last time in 1848.

To make better sense of a strange romance already told many times in the present tense, we turn first to the historical record to determine what we can learn about the family to which Poe wished to join his destiny.

The Powers were in Rhode Island almost from the beginning. There would be five Nicholas Powers in the family, the last of them Sarah Helen Whitman's father.

The first Nicholas Power received a home lot in Providence in 1640. He was in trouble briefly with the British authorities for trying to purchase Indian lands in Warwick (RI) — expressly forbidden in the treaties with the local tribes — and was "dismissed with an admonition."

Nicholas died in 1657, leaving his widow, Jane Power, a daughter, Hope, and the next Nicholas Power. This Nicholas died in the catastrophic King Phillip's War in 1675. He is not found in lists of combatants I examined, so he may have been killed in an Indian raid.

His son, Captain Nicholas Power, was born in 1673. This Nicholas's second wife was Mercy Tillinghast, daughter of the ominously-named Rev. Pardon Tillinghast. Captain Power died in 1734. (A divergent record indicates Anne Tillinghast as his wife and places his death at 1744.) This Captain Power was a merchant and distiller. He sold his estate and distillery in Dutch Guiana to Captain John Brown in 1743.

In the next generation, we have another Captain Nicholas Power, who was a merchant and rope-maker. He was married to Rebecca Corey, and died January 6, 1808. The records indicate he freed a Negro slave in 1781 (we hope it was the only such soul he "possessed.")

The Nicholas who figures in our story is the fifth, known as Nicholas Power, Jr., born September 15, 1771. He married Anna Marsh, daughter of Daniel and Susanna (Wilkinson)

<10>

Marsh on August 28, 1798 in Newport. Genealogical records indicate he was a merchant, going by the title of Major for some part of his life.

His mercantile life seemed to be land-locked: he formed a partnership as "Blodgett and Power" and opened a store near Providence's Baptist Meeting House. The goods sold there began with fabrics, linens, threads (English, Indian and Scottish), then dry goods, hardware and groceries. From 1808 to 1810 the store ran auctions of goods. Then, in 1812, the partnership terminated. The war with the British almost certainly interrupted their trade.

The genealogy records at The Providence Historical Society note, "He was absent from Providence much in later years." Helen Whitman's biographer Caroline Ticknor tells us that Nicholas Power took to sea to build back his fortune, and was captured by the British during the War of 1812.

He was not released until 1815, at which time he did not return to Providence. He was not seen or heard from in Rhode Island until around 1832 or 1833, when he made a sudden return to "make amends" and resume his family life. Indications are that his nineteen-year "widow" was aghast at his return and threw him out of the house. He took up residence in a Providence hotel, and, to the dismay of all, spent the years until his death on April 28, 1844, in conspicuous dissolution. In 1842, he got around to placing a marker on his mother's grave with an inscription lamenting the effect of his long absence on his parent's well-being. (Rebecca Corey Power had died in 1825, and it is likely that she never knew what became of her son).

This family history, with the particular details of paternal abandonment and irresponsibility, is important to our story.

<ɪɪ>

The Power Sisters

Nicholas and Anna's first child, Rebecca, was born in 1800. Sarah Helen Power, our and Poe's "Helen," was the second daughter, born in Providence on January 19, 1803. The house where she was born was that of her grandfather, Captain Nicholas Power, at the corner of South Main and Transit Streets. They lived in this house until her grandfather's death in 1808.

As the younger Nicholas Power's fortunes ebbed and flowed, the young family moved to a succession of houses and lodgings: a house at the corner of Snow and Westminster (now a parking lot in a depressed corner of downtown Providence); "the Grinnell House," and "the Angell Tavern," which had a garden leading to the water.

Sarah Helen's younger sister, Susan Anna, was born in 1813. Hers was a dark-shadowed life: daughter of a merchant euphemistically "lost at sea," she would mature into a willful manic-depressive, the classic mad relative without whom no New England house seemed complete.

After 1816, Mrs. Power purchased a house at 76 Benefit Street (now No. 88) as a residence for herself and her daughters. This was a splendid avenue perched on the hillside overlooking Providence's busy waterfront. It would be their home for more than four decades. The city's "College Hill" boasted fine mansions, classic churches and a small colonial burial ground just a few minutes' walk from their door (St. John's churchyard). The family was well able to live on the stocks and mortgages Mrs. Power had inherited from her mother, funds happily untouched by the impecunious Major Power.

Although Benefit Street was then fashionable, the street's origins would have pleased Edgar Poe's morbid tastes. The original settlers of Providence owned long, parallel strips of land starting at the river and running up over College Hill. Until 1710 or so, most families buried their dead on the hillside, and a lane that threaded among these family burial plots was what ultimately became Benefit Street. For many decades it remained a twisted street, bending round grave plots and old houses whose owners had not yet yielded the right-of-way,

<12>

way, until it finally became the straight avenue we know today. For some years, the street terminated with a gate, to ward off the denizens of the sinister North End.

To the north of Benefit Street, the 22-acre North Burial Ground was created in 1700, but the town's families did not begin burying the respectable dead there until 1711. With the creation of Benefit Street, the city fathers persuaded families to exhume and relocate their moldering ancestors to the North Burial Ground. (A few thrifty old families, it may be guessed, merely moved the gravestones.) A number of gloomy and derelict churchyards were also relocated there gradually, but St. John's churchyard remained, its wall abutting the Powers' rose garden.

Although a proper Providence upbringing in those days was probably rather stifling to the intellect, Helen had a few escapes during her younger years: she visited relatives on Long Island, New York and briefly attended a Quaker school. Despite the Puritanical suspicions and prohibitions of her relatives, she developed an early passion for poetry. She mastered Latin and would later be sufficiently adept in languages to read and translate both German and French.

In 1821, Sarah Helen's older sister Rebecca married William E. Staples. Two children were born to them in rapid succession. There is a Judge William Staples home just up the block from the Power house on Benefit Street, and this may be where the couple lived.

Despite her mother's deep-set mistrust of the male gender, Sarah Helen, too, was wooed and won away from the Benefit Street home. In 1824, during her twenty-first year, she was engaged to attorney John Winslow Whitman. Urged to assume the proper responsibilities of womanhood, Helen was pressured to put aside her literary ambitions. As her biographer Caroline Ticknor tells it, "Mrs. Whitman's taste for poetry was frowned upon by certain relatives...[She received] reproving letters, expressing the hope that she 'did not read much poetry, as it was almost as pernicious as novel-reading.'"

Mr. Whitman seemed a good match. He was not one of those lawyers whom Mr. Shakespeare would have us kill. The

<13>

third son of Massachusetts Judge Kilborne Whitman, he graduated from Brown University in 1818. He started a law practice in Boston, and practiced later in Barnstable.

During their long engagement, in 1825, Sarah Helen's grandmother, Rebecca Corey Power, died.

Sorrow struck again that year when Sarah Helen's older sister Rebecca died on September 14. She had been married only four years, and then her two children, according to the Power family records, "died young." Was her death childbirth-related, or did a contagion such as tuberculosis ("the galloping consumption") sweep through the Staples home, taking the young mother and then the children? This tragedy must have made a deep impression on the poetical Sarah Helen, who would have followed four coffins to the North Burial Ground in swift succession.

The Literary Helen Emerges

Sarah Helen's respectably-delayed marriage took place in 1828, with a Long Island wedding held on July 10 at the home of Sarah Helen's uncle, Cornelius Bogert. A four-year engagement may seem excessive by today's standards, but we can assume that Mr. Whitman also needed time to establish his law practice and set up a suitable home.

John Whitman turned out to have a creative side, too. It is interesting to note that Helen's biographers, and most of Poe's, seem to know Sarah Helen's husband only by his profession. I was startled to discover, during an Internet search, that John Winslow Whitman had another persona altogether: he was co-editor of *The Boston Spectator and Ladies' Album*. This journal published some of Sarah Helen's poems, under the name "Helen." Through her husband's Boston affiliations, she met and came to know the whole circle of Transcendentalists, and started writing and publishing essays on Goethe, Shelley and Emerson. Articles and poems in other magazines soon followed. Mrs. Whitman was clearly not going to vanish into the draperies, and she was fortunate to have a literary ally in her husband.

<14>

A few years later, a new kind of turmoil roiled the family. Sometime between 1831 and 1832, Sarah Helen's mother lost the right to wear her widow's bonnet, with the sudden reappearance of the wandering Nicholas Power. Did the Major return in a remorseful state, wanting to make amends and restore his family's fortune? Or was he ruined again, returning to old haunts to nibble away at his wife's property? Another legend has it that he had a second wife and family in the Carolinas, and had now abandoned them, too.

Sarah Helen, who had cherished a somewhat heroic image of her father, was crushed — and one can only imagine the effect of all this on the younger sister.

Like her father, Sarah Helen's husband was not destined for commercial success. Money vanished into failed inventions, and several business ventures went belly-up. Mr. Whitman even appears to have gone to jail for a few months in a legal upset involving a bad loan — not a happy career turn for a young attorney.

Worse yet, John Whitman also turned out to have a frail constitution. He caught colds frequently, and one of them, contracted in 1833, lingered and worsened into a total collapse and sudden death.

In 1833, then, Sarah Helen Whitman found herself a widow after only five years of marriage. She donned the official "widow's bonnet" and moved back in with her mother and younger sister on Benefit Street.

Although she would continue to be the dutiful daughter, Sarah Helen was now a published literary figure in her own right, confident in her worth and powers, and acquainted with many of the best minds of New England.

Meantime, Nicholas Power, rebuffed from the attractive red house on Benefit Street, had set up lodgings in a Providence hotel and began his new, disreputable existence, pursuing ladies of the theater. The prejudice against theater people was so strong in America at this time that actors were routinely forbidden the use of churches for weddings and funerals. So it is possible that the contemporary reference to "actresses" was a euphemism implying all kinds of women of the lower sort.

<15>

At this time, the Power-Whitman household probably assumed its frozen triangle of control, dependence and artistic defiance. One thinks of immobile Chekhov characters, locked in their parlor.

Mrs. Anna Power held the purse strings. She would make certain that no man ever got near the modest fortune that had come their way through the Marsh family.

Susan Anna careened between manic highs and long periods of sullen silence. One episode reportedly led her to a sanitarium stay, for "mania," but Mrs. Power evidently preferred the cheaper long-term solution of keeping her daughter at home, under constant supervision.

Mrs. Power probably established some stern rules about the extent to which Susan's mood swings would be humored — after her death, Sarah Helen seemed to surrender control to her reclusive "patient." In those latter years, during Susan's depressive periods, the house would be darkened and visitors turned away. Her need for silence, darkness and solitude were pampered, and if visitors were by some necessity admitted, Susan would hide in a closet. In her manic phases, Susan Anna collaborated on some well-wrought fairy-tale poems with Sarah Helen, and amused visitors with impromptu verses about the errant Nicholas Power.

Sarah Helen's outward personality had probably bloomed during her Boston days, and although she would accept the burden of living with her embittered mother, and helping to care for her sister, her mind, and her writing, were unfettered. She was with the gods — Goethe, Schiller, Shelley, Byron, Emerson. She studied occult lore and learned about mesmerism and spiritualism, as interest in these phenomena swept across the New England states. And when universal male suffrage, women's suffrage, and the abolition of slavery became New England's predominant issues, Sarah Helen was there. Seances, poetry and political activism, all went hand-in-glove.

An avid reader, she frequented the wonderful Providence Athenaeum, a membership lending library which opened its new Greek-revival temple only a few blocks away on Benefit Street in 1838. According to Jane Lancaster, the Athenaeum's

<16>

historian, there is no indication Helen was ever a member or "share holder" at the Athenaeum. I suspect her mother would not part with the cost of membership, so Sarah Helen borrowed books on the card of one of her Tillinghast relatives. She became a local celebrity, and parties and salons at her home drew not only the locals, but visiting celebrities such as Emerson. John Hay, a young poet later famed as Abraham Lincoln's secretary, was a devotee at the Power salon.

Sometime in 1838, Sarah Helen posed for a portrait, an oil painting by Giovanni Thompson that depicts her in a widow's cap with pink strings. This portrait of the 35-year-old poet occupies a place of honor in the Art Room of the Providence Athenaeum.

The Other Providence Poet: William Pabodie

In 1838, if not sooner, Sarah Helen would have made the acquaintance of William Jewett Pabodie, a Providence student who had been elected class poet by that year's graduating class of Brown University. He is of special interest since he plays a much-misunderstood role in the Poe-Helen romance.

Pabodie was making a name locally as a poet. He wrote a poem for the dedication of the Providence Athenaeum. He translated Goethe's "The Elf King" from the German. He declaimed his long poem, "Calidore," at the Brown graduation ceremony. Few listeners made it to the end of this forlorn Romantic poem of a drowned bride and a bereaved groom's suicide. A poem whose ending is littered with corpses is not an auspicious commencement piece, but it was Pabodie's *magnum opus* and he probably could not resist thrusting it upon the public.

Pabodie, doubtless with parental funding, immediately published *Calidore* as a book. He was parodied and mocked locally (one newspaper dubbed him "Mistress Nabodie.")

He tried throughout 1840 to get Providence's best families to subscribe to the founding of a literary magazine, which he intended to call *The Argosy: A Critical Journal of Literature and Art.* Two other prospective new journals had been spurned by

<17>

Providence in the preceding two years. When the first issue of the Transcendentalist journal *The Dial* appeared, Pabodie published an unfavorable sour-grapes newspaper review, saying, "the poetry scattered throughout the volume is generally of no high character." Pabodie's prospectus for his own magazine was mocked in a broadsheet that suggested he take up sewing instead of literature, a clear stab at his seeming lack of masculinity.

William Pabodie would remain on the Providence literary scene for decades, writing and publishing poetry. He did little else. Although he read at law and was admitted to the bar in 1838, he never took up the practice, and was essentially a "gentleman of leisure."

He also took up morphine and laudanum, and the pursuit of the poppy would go on till the end of his days. In his last decade he wrote no poetry at all. A look at his poetry, latter life and death leaves strong evidence that he was gay (then the most secret of secret societies). If you doubt this, go find his long prose poem with the refrain "Oh, sailor boy!" Or read the account of his lurid October 1870 suicide by ingesting Prussic Acid. Mrs Whitman noted that Pabodie had just inherited $100,000 that year, after the death of his brother.[1]

Further clues about Mr. Pabodie come from Helen herself, who seemed to distance herself from him after the Poe affair. She referred to Pabodie as "Poe's friend" rather than "my friend." Writing to Poe biographer John H. Ingram in 1874, she described Pabodie thus:

> He studied law, had a law office, & was a justice of the peace for several years, but he had an utter aversion to business, &, not being dependent on the profession for a support, soon abandoned it. He was a fine *belles lettres* critic, & has written a few very fine poems. Some of his patriotic & occasional odes have been quoted as among the noblest in our American literature. He was rather *super*fine in dress and manner, witty & sarcastic in conversation, very sensitive to the world's praise & blame, & *very* indolent[2].

[1] SHW, letter to Ingram, April 10, 1874, *Poe's Helen Remembers*, p. 114
[2] SHW, letter to Ingram, Nov. 27, 1874, *Poe's Helen Remembers*, p. 227

<18>

Literary New England in the 1840s

During these years, Sarah Helen maintained her place in a literary America that was exploding with new philosophical ideas. Despite the pious underpinnings of New England society, the 1840s were a decade of intellectual turmoil: end-of-the-world prophecies, new native religions, Brook Farm, the antislavery movement, spiritualism, and the restless intellectual odyssey of Emerson and the Transcendentalists. Science was advancing in leaps and bounds, and poets and essayists all felt that they had to take it all in and make sense of it.

Their problem was that they carried all the baggage of Platonic thought in a world that was becoming mechanistic and Aristotelian. It may seem strange to us that the same persons who read natural science and astronomy tomes also troubled themselves about souls, ghosts and Divinity. This is the complex world in which they lived. We can laugh at Transcendental abolitionists talking at seances to ghosts of dead Indians, but we do not have to look far to see equally bizarre belief-complexes among the intellectual class today.

The 1840s also represented a watershed for literacy and the appreciation of culture in America. Boston really was the Athens of the United States, and the roster of American writers active in mid-century was staggering. The Lyceum movement brought thousands of young people to hear writers and artists lecture, and lending libraries insured that working class people could have access to books. The prices of books were also falling dramatically during that period because of the introduction of the rotary printing press. Americans were proving to the world that high culture was for everyone. For an overview of literary America during this period, one of the best sources is still the classic book, *The Flowering of New England: 1815-1865,* by Van Wyck Brooks (E.P. Dutton, 1936).

In the early 1840s, Edgar Allan Poe had made his mark with stories, criticism, literary hoaxes and poems. His career was followed with interest, if not always approval, by his fellow critics. He had pretty much thrown the gauntlet against the New England *literati* in favor of the writers of New York

<19>

and points south, and he had even accused Longfellow of plagiarism.

At the end of June 1845, Poe was lured to Providence. A drunken Poe told his friend Thomas Holly Chivers on a Manhattan street, "I am in the damndest amour!" and said of the poet Mrs. Fannie Osgood, "I have just received a letter from her, in which she requests me to come on there this afternoon on the four o'clock boat." Poe, penniless, borrowed money for the journey, and was in Providence on or around July 1.

Fannie Osgood doubtless wanted to show off Poe on her rounds of social and literary visits. Possibly embarrassed by his empty pockets, his forlorn attire, and the uncertainty of his night's lodgings, Poe refused to be taken to Sarah Helen's house. (He may also have dreaded the Boston luminaries he might find there.) Instead, he wandered the streets of College Hill into the late hours.

Walking alone in the moonlight on Benefit Street, Poe recognized Helen's house from Mrs. Osgood's description, and caught a brief glimpse of the poet in her rose garden before she vanished into the rear of the house. It was a vision he could not forget. It is still possible to stand at the same corner today, peering into the same rose garden, hoping for a ghostly fluttering of Attic scarves and shawls.

Sarah Helen, for her part, was well aware of Poe in 1845. His magazine stories horrified and appalled her, yet she went back to them again and again. Poe's avowed belief in the power of souls to go back and forth from Death attracted her, and his poetry overwhelmed her. She wished to know him, yet knew from gossip from her friends, that he was scandal-prone, impoverished, and married to a young cousin whose declining health was his all-consuming concern. (Well, not *all*-consuming — here he was on the arm of the controversial New York poetess, scandalously separated from her painter husband.)

Meantime, Sarah Helen had settled into the eccentric style of dress and speech that Caroline Ticknor described thus: "deep-set eyes that gazed over and beyond, but never at you ...her movements were very rapid, and she seemed to flut-

<20>

ter like a bird. … Her spell was on you from the moment she appeared… when she spoke, her empire was assured. She was wise, she was witty … her quick, generous sympathy, her sweet, unworldly nature, her ready recognition of whatever feeble talent, or inferior worth another person possessed. … throughout her life she had a succession of adorers." Of her style, Ticknor tells us further, "[S]he loved silken draperies, lace scarves and floating veils … always shod in dainty slippers … [she] always carried a fan to shield her eyes from glare. Her rooms were always dimly lit."

The latter-day figure of Isadora Duncan comes to mind in this description, not surprisingly. Sarah Helen identified with Athena, so it was only natural that she should don the goddess' helmet for an occasional party. Poe biographers have made sport of Helen's appearance, describing how friends trailed her on the street, retrieving for her the various scarves and parts of her costume that always seemed to be falling off. Helen's pagan garb was pretty daring in a very conventional city.

Somewhere in these years, Sarah Helen also became convinced that she had a weak heart. By the time Poe came calling, she carried a tiny bottle of ether and a handkerchief with her at all times. Sniffing the ether was believed to ward off heart troubles; a more substantial dose guaranteed a convenient fainting swoon. Helen was able to fend off would-be husbands with this heart complaint, assuring them (and Poe as well) that while the exertions of the marriage bed might result in mutual ecstasy, for her this would also be certain death.

Helen had friendships that spanned Providence and New York. One of the New York poets known to Poe, Anne Lynch, was one of Helen's correspondents. From her and others, Sarah Helen had learned all about the consumption death of Virginia Poe in 1847, Edgar's own troubles, and his desperate poverty. She also made inquiries about whether Poe's seeming expertise in mesmerism was based on fact, since she was studying the literature on hypnotism with great enthusiasm. (This is back in the days when mesmeric influence was done with magnets as well as the waving of hands.)

Edgar Poe in New York

It is beyond the scope of the present book to outline the well-known biography of Poe. Our narrative, however, requires a knowledge of what Poe was up to during 1845 to 1849, the years in which his story and Helen's intertwine.

In 1845, Edgar Poe's personal, financial and romantic calamities piled one upon another in New York. Poe gained control of *The Broadway Journal* and secured financing for it. By late July his backer was referring to Poe as "a drunken sot." Poe's book of *Tales Grotesque and Arabesque*, meantime, was being reviewed everywhere, and the fame of his poem, "The Raven," flew throughout the states. In August, a visitor to the offices of *The Broadway Journal* found Poe "irascible, surly, and in his cups." In the August issue of the *Journal*, Poe reviewed a poem by Lowell and accused him of plagiarizing Wordsworth, and inaccurately quoted Wordsworth to prove it. Lowell wrote to Poe's partner that his editor lacked character, and got a commiserating letter back saying, "[Poe's] presumption is beyond the liveliest imagination." By the end of August, Poe was begging a $50 loan from Chivers to sustain the magazine.

On October 1, despite all these troubles, Poe sent the manuscript of *The Raven and Other Poems* off to the printer.

Poe managed to irritate the Boston literary world on October 16, when he was paid $50 to read a *new* poem as part of a Lyceum program. Unable to write anything new for the entire preceding month, Poe trekked to Boston and substituted "Al Aaraaf," a juvenile work, re-titling it "The Messenger Star." He did an encore reading of "The Raven." Then he went home and boasted in *The Broadway Journal* of having given Boston old goods. Reviews in Boston suggested that most of the audience fled before the poem was over, and numerous letters to journal editors pilloried Poe over his behavior.

Poe's tale, "The Facts in the Case of M. Valdemar," was circulated at this time under several titles in newspapers and magazines, and caused a stir in New England, where it was taken by many to be a factual account. It describes a man whose soul was retained after death through the power of hypnotism. The final sequence, in which Valdemar's body dissolves into

<22>

a putrescent mass when the hypnotic spell is broken, should have made it clear that this was a horror story. Sarah Helen Whitman, a student of mesmerism, wrote to friends in New York, begging to know whether Poe's story was true.

Sarah Helen would later write: "I can never forget the impressions I felt in reading a story of his for the first time … I experienced a sensation of such intense horror that I dared neither look at anything he had written nor even utter his name … By degrees this terror took the character of fascination — I devoured with a half-reluctant and fearful avidity every line that fell from his pen."

In October, Poe, with borrowed money, bought total ownership of *The Broadway Journal*. He then continued to beg friends and fellow authors for $50 loans.

By November 19, Poe had turned financial management of the *Journal* over to publisher Thomas H. Lane, retaining editorial control. That same day, Wiley & Putnam issued *The Raven and Other Poems*. By the end of month, Poe was begging a distant relative in Georgetown for a $200 loan.

In mid-December, Thomas Lane shut down *The Broadway Journal* after Poe vanished during a drinking binge, leaving the last issue of the magazine unfinished.

Poe was a brilliant editor and a feared critic, but he was clearly no businessman. In mid-1846 he was forced to flee to cheaper lodgings, moving along with his ailing wife and Mrs. Clemm, his mother-in-law, to a cottage at Fordham, The Bronx, 13 miles from lower Manhattan. By year's end, magazines and newspapers were describing the Poes as destitute and near starvation.

Poe's wife Virginia died of consumption on January 30, 1847. Later in the year, Poe won $225 in a libel suit, enjoyed the charity of the few New York literary ladies whom he had not offended, and published sketches of the New York *literati* in *Godey's Lady's Book*. He continued to live at Fordham with Mrs. Clemm ("Muddie"), Virginia's mother.

By November 1847, Poe's friends extracted the manuscript of "Ulalume" and persuaded a publisher to pay for it, so that the money might be used — to buy the poet *a pair of shoes*.

<23>

All the parties to the transaction pitied Poe, and all agreed they had no idea what the poem meant, despite its almost overwhelming beauty of language.

As 1848 began, Poe was busy writing his cosmological essay, *Eureka,* and drafting plans for his literary magazine, *The Stylus.* All he needed to launch his magazine, of course, was money.

The Year 1848 — Meetings and Calamities

Until very recently, most accounts of the Poe-Helen romance had essentially the same details, but often formed a vague chronology. "On one of Poe's visits..." we often read. Thanks to the latest in Poe scholarship, I have been able to collate, from several sources, a real chronological account of the Poe-Helen affair, with most of the dates in place. Just as we can best understand the psychology of Helen by tracing her whole family history, we can best understand the sometimes lunatic turns of the romance of the two poets only by putting things in order.

In the first edition of this book I discussed the affair in more general terms, content to let the reader do his or her own researches. Since then, my own fascination with the characters in this drama has deepened, and, having elaborated the Power family history in chronological order, let us plunge forward. (Thanks be to *The Poe Log: A Documentary Life of Edgar Allan Poe* compiled by Dwight Thomas and David K. Jackson, and to the clear-headed narrative of Kenneth Silverman in *Edgar A. Poe: Mournful and Never-ending Remembrance.*)

Although not all the events listed in the following pages may seem relevant, they all bear upon Poe's and Helen's state of mind during the year.

On January 1, 1848, *The Home Journal* reprinted Poe's poem "Ulalume," anonymously.

On February 3, Poe baffled a New York City lecture audience with his long, long talk titled "The Universe," his first

<24>

public presentation of his prose-poem *Eureka*. During the rest of his days, Poe would recite from his epic description of the creation and destruction of universes on the slightest pretext. He was convinced that he had "guessed" the deepest secrets of science, and he would expound to anyone who would listen (including drunks in taverns.) Poe's mammoth essay on astronomy and metaphysics has, as one of its final passages, the following:

> "No thinking being lives who, at some luminous point of his life of thought, has not felt himself lost amid the surges of futile efforts at understanding, or believing, that anything exists greater than his own soul. The utter impossibility of any one's soul feeling itself inferior to another; the intense, overwhelming dissatisfaction and rebellion at the thought; — these, with the omniprevalent aspirations at perfection, are but the spiritual, coincident with the material, struggles towards the original Unity — are, to my mind at least, a species of proof far surpassing what Man terms demonstration, that no one soul is inferior to another — that nothing is, or can be, superior to any one soul — that each soul is, in part, its own God — its own Creator: — in a word, that God — the material and spiritual God — now exists solely in the diffused Matter and Spirit of the Universe; and that the regathering of this diffused Matter and Spirit will be but the re-constitution of the purely Spiritual and Individual God."

This woolly pantheism is an odd song for a writer who mocked Emerson and the New England thinkers. It is also patently blasphemous against the views of everyday Christians. Poe's book may in part be a response to a popular book published in 1840, which I found nestled on the open stacks of The Providence Athenaeum — Thomas Dick's *The Sidereal Heavens, and other Subjects Connected with Astronomy, as Illustrative of the Character of the Deity, and of an Infinity of Worlds*. This volume was indicative of the vain attempt to make observed science fit

<25>

the Scriptures. Poe's version turns the churchgoers' cosmos inside out, but is ultimately just as ridiculous as its inspiration.

In January 1848, Mrs. Lynch invited Sarah Helen to contribute poetic greetings to a Valentine's Day party she was planning for the New York *literati*. Helen and her sister Susan both sent poems. Helen's was addressed to Poe.

Only after the February 14 party was over did Sarah Helen learn that Poe had not been invited, and was now in fact *persona non grata* among much of the literary set (certain people would not attend if they knew Poe was invited, *etc. etc.*). Anne Lynch then submitted 42 poems that had been read at her party for publication in the *Home Journal*. Helen's poem was not among them.

It took two more communications to a reluctant Anne Lynch to get her to pass along the Poe valentine for publication. The *Home Journal* published it separately. Although the poem as originally written is a clear "come hither," common friends assured Poe that Helen was dour and eccentric. None of these friends mentioned to Poe, perhaps intentionally, that Helen was a widow.

Sarah Helen revised her valentine poem substantially in later years, making its imagery encompass more of Poe's writing. Since it is the poem that launched the love affair, I have included both versions in this edition. The original valentine is titled "To. E.A. Poe," and the revised poem is titled "The Raven."

Poe's most recent biographer, Kenneth Silverman, in his book *Edgar A. Poe: Mournful and Never-Ending Remembrance,* is the first to acknowledge that Helen was a formidable match for Poe intellectually. Unlike the dilettante ladies Poe knew in New York, Silverman observes, "Sarah Helen Whitman was a woman with sophisticated philosophical and literary interests — after her friend Margaret Fuller, perhaps the leading female literary critic in America." He lists the depth of her literary studies, and her love of Goethe, Shelley, Shakespeare and the Transcendentalists. He adds, intriguingly, "She also studied mesmerism and magnetic science, of which Providence was a center. Convinced that an Other World existed, she went be-

<26>

yond both Emerson and Mesmer in the pursuit of occult knowledge."

At the time I assembled the first edition of this book, there were no Poe biographers making such generous assertions about Sarah Helen's worth. Instead, she was more often mocked as a poetess swooning with her ether-soaked handkerchief.

Only after interrogating other literary women by letter did Poe learn that "Mrs." Whitman was a widow. Fanny Osgood wrote to Helen, warning her with some humor that the New York raven would certainly descend on the Providence dove.

Two Women in Lowell

Poe, who was beginning to thrash about for female companionship to center his life, was already commencing a long distance relationship with the first of two women in Lowell, Massachusetts.

The first was Jane Locke, who lured Poe to the mill city for a paid lecture and reading. In correspondence, Jane Locke sounded like a potential soul-mate, but her fevered letters were worded so cautiously that Poe could not ascertain her age, or even whether she was single, married, or a widow.

While still trying to figure out Jane Locke's status, Poe responded to Sarah Helen's "come hither" poem by tearing a page from one of his printed books — his early poem "To Helen" which was inspired by Helen Stanard, a married lady Poe was obsessed with in his youth. He sent the poem anonymously on March 2.

Then, in May, with the Muse on his side, Poe penned the longer prose-poem "To Helen," which recollected the vision of Sarah Helen seen in her rose garden that summer night three years earlier. He mailed it anonymously to Helen on June 1. She matched its handwriting to the address of the envelope containing the earlier poem. A friend confirmed for her that it was indeed Poe's handwriting. She sent two stanzas of her own verse to Poe, with hints of encouragement.

As summer commenced, Poe was getting desperate to sort the ladies out. He was preparing his lecture for the mysterious Jane Locke in Lowell. At least he could investigate Sarah Helen

<27>

long-distance. He wrote poet Anna Blackwell, who had recently been in Providence for "magnetic therapy," asking "Can you not tell me something about her — anything — every thing you know — and let no one know that I have asked you to do so?"

In Lowell, Massachusetts, Poe gave his scheduled performance on July 10 — his new talk, "The Poets and Poetry of America." He included special praise for the poetry of Mrs. Whitman. He tried not to appear quite so shocked as he was, when he discovered that his professed "soul mate," Jane Locke, was a 43-year-old married women with five children. Mrs. Locke, after showing off the visiting poet to the other mill owners' wives, would later give birth to an ecstatic long poem deifying Poe — the only fruit of her intended union with the famous writer.

During the Lowell visit, though, lightning struck. As he was dragged around to the Lockes' relatives, Poe met the "other" woman: 28-year-old Nancy "Annie" Richmond. Poe fled the threatened embraces of Mrs. Locke, and stayed over at the Richmonds' home in Westford. That night, he fell hopelessly in love (Platonic, brotherly love, of course) with "Annie," who in- stantly became his sister, twin, goddess — almost enough to push the lamented Virginia out of the cosmos. One could almost hear Virginia's ghost, coughing tubercularly, outside the Richmonds' parlor.

"Annie" was conveniently married to an indulgent paper mill owner who didn't seem to mind his wife entertaining and corresponding with a harmless, broken-down poet. Annie's three-year-old daughter, far from daunting to Poe, seemed an angel next to the pawing horde of little Lockes.

Since the Richmonds were related to the Lockes, one can only imagine the repercussions of this poetic abduction, especially after Poe began inundating Annie with letters.

Back in New York, Poe's book *Eureka* was issued by Putnam's. Poe had tried to convince the skeptical publisher that this landmark book would be so popular that presses would run day and night to keep it in stock. *Eureka* was then, and

<28>

may now still be, the least-read book by any major American writer.

In late July, Poe was off to Richmond to try to raise funds for his long-dreamt-of magazine, *The Stylus.* There, he distinguished himself with a two-week drinking binge, incoherent visits to editors, a thwarted duel, and a reacquaintance with a lady named Elmira Royster. She is outside the ken of our story here, except that Poe *almost* proposed to her. It seemed a fatality of Poe's that the further South he went, the closer to doom he came.

While he was in Virginia, Helen's two stanzas of poetry arrived. The lines were encouraging — she had *read* — she had *understood*. He may have sensed that the sterner, more sober lifestyle of New England was what he really needed. Perhaps Sarah Helen would be his salvation — if not, the divine Annie was near. Poe hurtled back northward.

Poe Arrives in Providence

On Thursday, September 21, 1848 — an equinoctial, portentous date — Edgar Poe arrived in Providence, after devising a letter of introduction so that he could present himself to Mrs. Whitman in person.

On Friday, September 22, Poe and Helen toured a cemetery — purportedly Swan Point Cemetery. Some have questioned whether Poe and Helen ventured all the way to the then-rural Swan Point, more than three miles' walk through dirt lanes and woods. Originally I was inclined to doubt this, too. The Episcopal Churchyard of St. John's, just yards from Sarah Helen's door, was one candidate, but prying eyes were everywhere there. The North Burial Ground, Providence's traditional cemetery, was closer, and would have given her a chance to show Poe her relatives' graves, as well as the stones of some of Providence's founding fathers. But Swan Point, which had opened just two years earlier, was American's second "garden cemetery," and everyone was curious to see the new idea in landscaped, park-like cemeteries, even if the spot

<29>

was not yet full of the neglected graves and crumbling old mausoleums that Helen's recollections seem to suggest.

It is my opinion that they may have gone to the North Burial Ground, and that Helen romanticized the story by saying, years later, that they had gone to Swan Point. We do know, though, that Poe was avid about long walks, and Helen would have been grateful for the chance to talk about poetry and friendship away from the eyes and ears of mother and sister. If so, she must have come home late, exhausted, speechless, her shawls and scarves full of burrs, to the alarm of Mrs. Power.

If she smiled a quiet smile and refused to say much, it was understandable. In a secluded spot in the cemetery, Poe had put his arm around her waist and proposed marriage.

Poe stayed on until Sunday, September 24. Presumably, in those days, he met some of Helen's other friends, including the poetic Mr. Pabodie. Poe and Pabodie had much in common — both were poets with a leaning toward the hyper-romantic, funereal and supernatural; both detested the Boston literati; and both had dreams of founding a national literary journal. Pabodie had much to gain if Poe and Helen, his friends, remained in Providence and launched *The Stylus*.

As Poe learned just how close Sarah Helen still was to the New England literary circle, he grew alarmed: her friends were emphatically not his. He also learned that Helen was known to the whole circle of New York literary women, and could thus expect to receive letters from the likes of Mrs. Ellet, his social nemesis in New York. He began earnestly to warn Helen that his very real detractors would do anything they could to thwart his — and their — mutual happiness. Even more so would the envious mediocrities oppose the union of two poetic *geniuses*.

Because of transportation difficulties, Poe remained in Providence yet another day. On Monday morning, September 25 he went alone to Swan Point Cemetery. His train for New York was not until 6:00 in the evening. If this is actually what he did with his day, the long walk, similar to those he enjoyed during his better New York period, would have given him ample time to reflect on his potential new life. What he made of Mrs. Power and her moody sister Susan Anna, and how he

<30>

thought the Poe-Whitman household would take shape, were doubtless foremost in his mind. Could Helen be persuaded to leave Providence and move with him to New York, where they would found *The Stylus* and begin their joint triumph over the kingdom of letters? Or would he move to Rhode Island and clean the Augean stables of the Transcendentalists?

Back in New York City, on September 30, Poe received Helen's letter declining his proposal. Family duties, age differences, her health and other unstated issues were insurmountable, she said. And indeed, she had begun to hear unsettling things about him…

October arrived, and on its first day Poe worked up a proper fury writing his first love letter to Helen. On October 18, he wrote another one. They are his longest, most impassioned letters, and they have been reprinted numerous times in Poe biographies.

In late October (the dates here are not certain), Poe was back in Providence again, asking Helen to reconsider her refusal. This is likely the time they spent showing one another their poetry and best work, especially in the shadowed nooks of the Athenaeum, away from Mother's rebuking glances. Now Poe worked his magic, trying to convince her she was not too old, nor too frail, to be the companion who would save his soul. And he appealed to her as an artist, challenging her to the level of *ambition* required to join the immortals.

Since it seemed in Edgar Poe's character to do the worst thing always, he appeared at Helen's house more than once in an obvious state of inebriation. Perhaps Mr. Pabodie also introduced Poe to the pubs in Providence's notorious North End, where sailors brawled and where the police frequently raided "common brothels" and "brothels of the lowest sort."

His counter-arguments made, Poe then secured Helen's promise that she would write to him with her reply.

<31>

Another Interval with the Richmonds

Things in Lowell did not turn out as planned. Poe found his first pretext to leave Mrs. Locke's home and become a guest of the Richmonds once again in nearby Westford. The sympathetic Annie Richmond showered Poe with sympathetic and sisterly affection, and Poe doubtless shared with her all his doubts and worries about the proposal to Helen. She may have counseled him to persevere in the marriage, knowing how desperately he needed a center for his life. Poe walked to the post office daily, looking for Helen's letter, and was miserable each day when it did not appear.

The planned Lowell lecture was canceled because of the distractions leading up to the 1848 Presidential election (possibly the lecture hall became unavailable). Poe thus lost a desperately needed lecture fee.

One consolation was a three-day visit to Westford, Massachusetts, where Annie Richmond's parents hosted Poe and Annie, and Poe was induced to read for an appreciative local audience. On one of these days, Poe took a long, solitary walk in the hilly countryside.

Poe's presence in the Richmond home finally provoked the festering jealousy of Mrs. Locke. Open hostilities broke out between the Lockes and the Richmonds. By this time, the indulgent Mr. Richmond was doubtless alerted that something was improper about Poe's attentions to his wife.

Around November 2, Helen finally wrote a brief, vague letter, which Poe received in Lowell, neither confirming nor denying the idea of an engagement, and this letter agitated Poe even more. On Friday, November 3, he sent back a note indicating he would be in Providence on Saturday. He now stood to lose the links to both of his New England women, the poetic bride and the Platonic sister-spirit.

Annie continued to encourage him in the marriage to Mrs. Whitman. Poe, in great turmoil, agreed to renew his courtship in Providence, but got Annie to promise that she would come to him if he were near death.

<32>

Laudanum and Ultima Thule

On Saturday, November 4, Poe arrived in Providence. Helen waited at her home, and Poe never arrived. Instead he spent what he called "a long, long, hideous night of despair." It is hard to credit his claim that he spent the night alone in his hotel room. If there was any time he needed a drink, it was now...

Sunday dawned, and Poe decided that he would return to the city of his birth, Boston. He would kill himself, and summon Annie to be at his side for his final moments. Here is how he related it to Annie in a letter written two weeks later:

> I arose & endeavored to quiet my mind by a rapid walk in the cold, keen air — but all *would* not do — the demon tormented me still. Finally I procured two ounces of laudanum & without returning to my Hotel, took the cars back to Boston. When I arrived, I wrote you a letter, in which I opened my whole heart to you — to *you* — my Annie, whom I so madly, distractedly love — I told you how my struggles were more than I could bear — how my soul revolted from saying the words which were to be said [proposing marriage once again to Mrs. Whitman]— and that not even for your dear sake, could I bring myself to say them. I then reminded you of that holy promise, which was the last I exacted from you in parting — the promise that, under all circumstances, you would come to me on my bed of death — I implored you to come *then* — mentioning the place where I should be found in Boston — Having written this letter, I swallowed about half the laudanum & hurried to the Post Office — intending not to take the rest until I saw you — for, I did not doubt for one moment, that my *own* Annie would keep her sacred promise — But I had not calculated on the strength of the laudanum, for, before I reached the Post Office my reason was entirely gone, & the letter was never put in.

<33>

Monday, November 6th was a lost day. In Boston, a good Samaritan helped Poe, quite out of his mind, to find and board the train, not to Lowell and Westford, but back to Providence.

On Tuesday morning, November 7, Poe came to the Power house on Benefit Street early in the morning and demanded to see Helen. Helen sent word through a servant that she would see him at noon. Poe insisted to the servant that he had to see Helen at once, because he had an engagement later. Rebuffed, Poe went back to his hotel and scribbled a note that read:

> I have *no* engagements, but am *very* ill — so much so that I must go home, if possible — but if you say 'stay', I will try & do so. If you cannot see me — write me *one word* to say that you *do* love me and that, *under all circumstances,* you will be mine. Remember that these coveted words you have never yet spoken… It was not in my power to be here on Saturday as I proposed…

Helen met Poe later that morning at the Athenaeum. Helen accepted Poe's explanation that he had taken laudanum to "calm himself" and had suffered an overdose. He chided her for delaying her letter to Lowell for so long, and urged her to marry him immediately and return with him to New York.

The next day, Wednesday, November 8, the two poets had recovered their equilibrium. Now it was Helen's turn to balk. She had received several letters from New York cautioning her about Poe and his drinking. Helen herself later wrote:

> [H]e had vehemently urged me to an immediate marriage. As an additional reason for delaying a marriage which, under any circumstances, seemed to all my friends full of evil portents, I read to him some passages from a letter which I had recently received from one of his New York associates. He seemed deeply pained and wounded by the result of our interview, and left me abruptly saying that if we met again, it would be as strangers.

<34>

Helen assumed that Poe, who had written her a tortured farewell note from his hotel, had taken the evening train to New York. But Poe was going nowhere. He may not even have had the train fare. Instead he spent the evening in the bar-room of his hotel. We can imagine "The Raven" and "Eureka" intoned, others paying for the visiting celebrity's drinks, and the refrain of "Nevermore!" shaking the rafters. We can imagine Poe in his cups, reading the one poem certain to make him think of Virginia … and what might he have said, in his bitterness, about the dainty widow on the hill? And Mr. Pabodie was always about, making us wonder, too, where Poe obtained his laudanum.

Helen passed a night of "unspeakable anxiety in thinking what might befall him traveling alone in such a state of mental perturbation and excitement."

Sometime during the night, a man named MacFarlane attached himself to the miserable poet, and saw him through the night. In the morning, MacFarlane dragged him to Masury & Hartshorn's daguerreotype parlor, where Poe permitted himself to be immortalized in his misery. This is the famous "Ultima Thule" portrait, showing Poe with his face distorted — the lingering after-effect of the drug overdose, combined with the emotional crises which had accumulated upon him.

It was the morning of Thursday, November 9. Helen wrote: "He came alone to my mother's house in a state of wild and delirious excitement calling upon me to save him from some terrible impending doom. The tones of his voice were appalling and rang through the house. Never have I heard anything so awful, awful even to sublimity." It would not be too far a stretch to guess that Poe had taken another laudanum "calmative," for this behavior does not sound like a mere hangover.

Poe stayed in the house for several hours. When Helen finally had the nerve to enter the parlor, Poe hailed Helen as an angel and clung to her, tearing away a piece of muslin. A doctor was summoned, and brain congestion was the diagnosis. Mr. Pabodie was on hand, and as a devotee of the poppy, he might have known a lot more about Poe's condition than the

<35>

doctor. Poe was removed to Pabodie's house, where he lodged for a few days.

By November 13, Sarah Helen felt that Poe was himself again. He seemed to have worked an almost mesmeric spell over her. They went together to the daguerreotype parlor and had Poe photographed. At this point, to everyone's astonishment, Helen agreed to a conditional engagement, provided that Poe pledged to absolutely refrain from drinking. If Poe behaved as a model suitor, she hoped to persuade her mother to approve the marriage, perhaps as soon as December. Satisfied, Poe left on the six o'clock train for Stonington, from where he would get the steamer boat to New York.

Within hours, Helen and her mother heard some gossip about Poe's recent conduct — possibly an account of how much and how often he had imbibed while in Providence, and only blocks from the Benefit Street home. These new reports "augmented almost to phrenzy" Mrs. Power's opposition to the union. Helen's response was to scan the heavens and write the first of her poems "To Arcturus."

Engaged, But Full of Foreboding

On November 14, Poe was reinstalled at the cottage at Fordham. He and Helen exchanged more letters. Poe called Helen "beloved of my heart, of my imagination, of my intellect" but added ominously, "I am calm and tranquil and but for a strange shadow of coming evil which haunts me I should be happy. That I am not supremely happy, even when I feel your dear love at my heart terrifies me. What can this mean?"

By late November, other missives were flying. Mrs. Anne Lynch in New York wrote to William Pabodie to ask if the rumors of the Edgar Poe-Helen Whitman engagement were true. Fannie Osgood rushed to Providence and called on Sarah Helen. Unlike the others, she defended Poe. As Sarah Helen later recalled, "She threw herself at my feet & covered my hands with tears & kisses; she told me all the enthusiasm that she had felt for him & her unchanged and unchanging interest in him & his best welfare."

<36>

Poe, for his part, spent November writing Helen several long letters detailing the vengeful nature of his enemies on the New York literary scene. He convinced Helen of their frenzied desire to do him harm.

Sometime after December 7, Poe had returned to Providence. On December 12, Poe sat with Helen and read her long poem, "Hours of Life." If he had any doubts about her poetic worth, or the quality of her mind, he now knew he had a formidable mate. He urged her to complete the poem and publish it as soon as possible. On one of these evenings, Poe and Helen sat silently on opposite sides of the Power parlor. Helen stood, as if under a hypnotic power, and walked to the center of the room, where Poe embraced her. They kissed, and then Helen went to sit at Poe's side. All this without a word spoken.

Poe returned by train and steamer to Fordham. His late wife's mother, Mrs. Clemm, had to be prepared for the news, and it is likely that Poe did not have the money in pocket to remain day after day in a hotel, not to mention the daily expenses of a courtship.

Seeing that Helen was determined to marry Poe, the Power clan swung into action. On Friday, December 15, Mrs. Power, consulting with Charles F. Tillinghast, administrator of the Marsh estates, drew up an agreement in which Helen transferred all her money and property to her mother. This would prevent Poe from having any access to the family estate and funds. Sarah Helen dared not oppose her mother, and wrote to Poe and Mrs. Clemm with this unpleasant news.

Poe's reply to Helen was reassuring. On Saturday, December 16 he wrote:

> My *own dearest* Helen — Your letters — to my mother & myself — have just been received & I hasten to reply … I cannot be in Providence until Wednesday morning and, as I must try and get some sleep after I arrive, it is more than probable that I shall not see you until about 2, P.M. Keep up heart
> — *for all will go well.* My mother sends her dearest

<37>

love and says she will return good for evil & treat
you *much* better than *your* mother has treated me.

While visiting poet Mary E. Hewitt in New York City, Poe expressed a very different opinion about whether the intended marriage was going to happen. He told her, repeating his words twice for emphasis, "That marriage will never take place."

On Wednesday, December 20, Poe arrived early in the morning and checked into the Earl House at 67 North Main Street. At 7:30, Poe delivered his Franklin Lyceum lecture at Howard's Hall, to an audience of 1800 to 2000 persons. Sarah Helen sat in the front row. His lecture, "The Poetic Principle," showed Poe at his best. He also read "The Raven" and the early version of "The Bells."

That night, flush with success and with his speaker's fee in pocket, Poe fell in with a group of dissolute young men at his hotel (so Pabodie described them, and we suspect he knew them). They persuaded the famous poet to drink with them. And with Poe, that meant drink after drink, and choruses of "Nevermore!"

On Friday, December 22, Poe arose in his hotel. He dressed and went out for breakfast, but *the hotel bar was already open.* So he went in and had a glass of wine. Who would know?

At Helen's home a little later, Poe was required to sign the Power family property transfer agreement as a witness. It must have been a moment of supreme humiliation. Pabodie also signed the agreement as a witness. It was now plain that if he married Helen, she would go with him to Fordham as a penniless woman with a trunk full of clothes and books. If he broke off the engagement at this point, he would be branded forever as a fortune hunter and a man without honor.

The arrangements continued with grim determination. The pace suddenly accelerated: Mr. Pabodie was asked to contact the minister and make official arrangements for a Monday, December 25 wedding. The process of "publishing the banns" meant that the intended marriage was to be announced on Sunday in the church in the week preceding the marriage. In earlier times, the banns were announced three weeks in

<38>

succession, during which period anyone in the congregation had a chance to raise objections, legal or moral.

Pabodie put the note from Poe to the minister in his pocket but did not deliver it to St. John's church, which was a stone's throw from the Whitman house. Was this at Poe's request? Or was this done in connivance with Mrs. Power? Or were they all, Sarah Helen included, going through motions they wished some Providential force would interrupt?

Poe seemed to treat the marriage as a certainty. He sent off a note to Mrs. Clemm that read "We shall be married on Monday [Christmas Day], and will be at Fordham on Tuesday, in the first train." If a Christmas Day wedding sounds unlikely to modern readers, I am assured from a perusal of Stephen Nissembaum's *The Battle for Christmas* that New England was decades away from marking Christmas as a cardinal church or state holiday. A Christmas Day wedding was not, therefore, objectionable or unusual, but it was certainly sudden.

At the Athenaeum, Revelations

Oppressed by the atmosphere of the Power house, Poe and Sarah Helen fled to the quietude of The Athenaeum. There, nestled amid the dimly-lit stacks, the two poets sat together. Both of them were beleaguered by events, and human nature being what it is, they may have been even more resolved to make the whole thing work. Life in New York would be difficult, but Poe was famous, a sworn reformed man, and they both had many friends there.

This was the moment, as in every Greek drama, when a messenger arrives with disastrous news. A messenger boy ran into the Athenaeum, breathless, asking for Mrs. Whitman. He handed her a letter. It was urgent, he said, that she read it at once. She opened the envelope and read in silence.

I will let Helen tell the rest of what transpired a little later back at the Power house:

<39>

View of Providence and College Hill, 1844.

The Power family home on Benefit Street. The Poe-Whitman courtship took place in this house. The famous rose garden described in the poem "To Helen" is behind the house, whose back wall overlooks St. John's Churchyard.

St. John's Church in Providence, side view. The church, until recently Providence's main Episcopal cathedral, fronts on North Main Street. The wall at the back of the churchyard is below Benefit Street. Benefit Street was paved over a number of old family grave plots, whose occupants were moved to the North Burial Ground.

The Providence Atheneaum on Benefit Street opened in 1838, a successor to two older member-supported libraries dating back to 1753. Poe and Mrs. Whitman met here, and Poe signed out books from the library during his stay in the city.

Recollect — we were to be married in a few days. Poe had at last prevailed upon me to consent to an immediate union. He had written to Dr. Crocker to publish the "banns of marriage" between us. He had written to Mrs. Clemm to announce our arrival in New York early in the following week, when it came to my knowledge & the knowledge of my friends, that he had already broken the solemn pledge so lately given by taking wine or something stronger than wine at the bar of his hotel. No token of this infringement of his promise was visible in his appearance or his manner, but I was at last convinced that it would be in vain longer to hope against hope. I knew that he had irrevocably lost the power of self-recovery.

Gathering together some papers which he had entrusted to my keeping, I placed them in his hands without a word of explanation or reproach, and, utterly worn out & exhausted by the mental conflicts & anxieties of the last few days, I drenched my handkerchief in ether & threw myself on a sofa, hoping to lose myself in utter unconsciousness. Sinking on his knees beside me, he entreated me to speak to him-one word, *but one word.* At last I responded almost inaudibly, "What can I say?" "Say that you love me, Helen." *"I love you."*

Those three words were the last I ever spoke to him. He remonstrated & explained & expostulated. But I had sunk from a violent ague fit into a cold and death-like stupor. He brought shawls and covered me with them, & then lifting me in his arms, bore me to a lounge near the fire, where he remained on his knees beside me, chafing my hands & invoking me, by all tenderest names & epithets, to speak to him again, *one* word. A merciful apathy was now stealing over my senses, & though I vaguely heard all, or much, that was said, I spoke no word, nor gave any sign of life. My mother & sister & another friend

<42>

I heard my mother remonstrating with him &
urging his departure.

Then Mr. Pabodie entered the room and joined my
mother in entreaties that he would leave me. Her last
words I did not hear, but I heard him haughtily and
angrily reply, "Mr. Pabodie, you hear how I am
insulted." These were his last words, & the door
closed behind him forever. His letters I did not dare
to answer. Exaggerated and humiliating stories were in
circulation. He entreated me to deny them, to say that
I at least had not authorized them. I never answered
the letter.[1]

Within days, everyone knew, from Providence to New
York, how Poe had courted and lost the poetic Mrs. Whitman.
Each telling of the scene in the parlor became more melodra-
matic, until it finally seemed that the militia had been called to
remove the deranged poet from the premises. Meanwhile, to
the mortification of all parties, newspapers all over the Northeast noted the impending nuptials, one of them even looking
forward to a clan of little Poes.

What was *really* in the letter that made Helen break off the
engagement? Helen discreetly said it was about Poe's glass of
wine in his hotel that morning, but it was probably a litany of
all of Poe's recent transgressions, gathered by a loose conspir-
acy of vagrants, snitches, Temperance bar-watchers, and maybe
even an off-duty police officer or two. An artist could have
dashed off sketches from the Poe daguerreotype, facilitating a
near-total "Poe watch" in the neighborhood. Any words that
Poe uttered in his drinking escapades might also have been
repeated. (Almost all of Poe's biographers have marveled at the
flow of gossip in Providence, so I'm making the leap to guess
that Helen was given an unvarnished précis of Poe's activities.)

Thus it is hard to avoid feeling that Poe was being watched,
probably from the time he was photographed on November 9.
Poe also had the distinct feeling that he was being followed and
watched all the way back to New York.

Some Poe biographers have assumed that the fatal missive
contained details about Poe's squabbles with the lady poets in

---

[1] SHW, letter to Ingram, May 1, 1874. *Poe's Helen Remembers*, p. 145.

< 43 >

New York, but he had already told her about that. Others suggest she received a letter about Annie Richmond — but Helen did not know about the simultaneous letters to Annie until almost thirty years later. More likely, the letter was all the local gossip someone had gathered on Mrs. Powers' behalf, if not at her behest.

Sarah Helen remained silent about the whole affair. Later, she published a poem to tell Poe indirectly of her undying affection for him. Poe, for his part, may have written "Annabel Lee" to memorialize their romance. But before they could ever meet again, Poe was found in a stupor on a Baltimore street during the crazed days of a local election. He died, drifting between lucidity and delirium, on October 7, 1849.

Sarah Helen Whitman lived for three more decades. In 1853, she published the poems she had written to and about Poe. In 1860, two years after the death of her mother, she published *Edgar Poe and His Critics,* a small but well-reasoned defense of Poe's writing and reputation. Although she seldom left Providence, she published her poems in major magazines and newspapers, and maintained correspondence with writers around the world. Her loyalty to Poe and her unselfish help to Poe biographers over the decades helped turn the tide of popular opinion against those who had slandered him. Helen's achievement is one of the great vindications in literary history.

In the years until 1860, Helen was generally silent about her relationship with Poe. She relied upon friends to defend her honor — and Poe's. After the infamous "memoir" of Poe published by Rufus Griswold circulated wild and exaggerated stories about Poe and his conduct, William Pabodie published a letter in *The New York Tribune* in 1852, refuting some of Griswold's libelous and distorted history. When Griswold threatened Pabodie with a libel suit in return, Pabodie defied him and published another letter showing further falsehoods in Griswold's writing. (It is a touching irony that Griswold's later life would be ruined by Mrs. Ellet, who had herself been Poe's nemesis among the literary women of New York.)

<44>

Helen Whitman remained in touch with Mrs. Clemm, Poe's mother-in-law, and sent her many gifts of money over the years. She became a devoted correspondent to Poe's admirers and biographers, both in America and overseas.

After Mrs. Power's death in 1858, Helen and her sister purchased another house, which was moved in the 20th century from its original location to 140 Power Street. The home was Sarah Helen's literary salon. It was also a sanitarium for her sister. Susan Anna Power, who seems to have drifted into religious mania, lived until December 8, 1877. Sarah Helen Whitman fell ill shortly after her sister's death, and was moved to the home of friends on Bowen Street, where she died June 27, 1878.

Helen continued all her life to defend Poe's honor and reputation. She did not learn the details of Poe's letters to Annie Richmond, and how exactly contemporaneous they were with Poe's courtship of her, until her last year, when John Henry Ingram published a group of Poe's "Annie" letters. It was a bitter discovery.

The Imp of the Perverse

Biographies of Poe make him either saint or monster. The monstrous image got its impetus from the exaggerations if not calumnies of the Reverend Rufus Griswold, who libeled Poe after his death, even while acting as his literary executor. Other literati whom Poe had criticized and mocked in his reviews joined forces with the society of spurned "literary ladies" to cement the present-day image of Poe as a drunkard, perennial drug addict, and less-than-honorable suitor.

Overzealous admirers, on the other hand, would have us believe that Poe never took a drink, told a lie, or felt a dishonorable affection. The need to "whitewash" literary figures may be hard for today's readers to understand. We are not that far away from a time when the right sort of people did not read books written by the wrong sort of author. The works of Poe,

<45>

Shelley, Lord Byron and Walt Whitman were all banned from homes and libraries as much for the behavior or demeanor of the authors as for the content of the works.

The fight for Poe's reputation, therefore, began with a kindly motive: to fight for his place in the history of our literature. But the time for sanitizing is long since over — today we want the whole man, blemishes and all. With Poe this is a challenge because the worst has already been said about him, and we must sort out what to believe and what to discard. The Poe-Helen narrative is especially troublesome since we are forced here to examine Edgar Allan Poe during a period of troubled decline.

An artist of Poe's intellect, passion and imagination was by necessity an outsider to convention. In Poe we see a man of brilliance and integrity who was nonetheless driven by his passions to dangerous contradictions.

His flirtations with the literary women of his day are perfect examples of his contradictory nature. There is nothing more typical of the poetic impulse than to fall into an abstract, other-worldly infatuation with someone unattainable. Poe attracted the attentions of a number of women poets. In the hothouse society they frequented, they all met and competed for the attention of the real poetic lions. They wrote valentines and structured acrostic verses around their names and initials. They encouraged passionate, personal letters.

This might seem to the jaded modernist a mere prelude to adultery. In Poe's case these poetic flatteries were likely the only "embraces" actually exchanged. Some of Poe's friendships with his lady poets were conducted in the full presence and acquiescence of amused husbands and other family members. To Poe, the lady poets were sensitive and clever, but hardly serious. Their poems and letters to him were praise; his to them, flattery and gallantry. In both types of exchanges, hyperbole was expected.

This is not to say that Poe's affections for various women, including Sarah Helen Whitman, were unreal. Poe seems even to have understood how this aloof literary and intellectual passion would be his battery. An early poem, "Romance," rather

<46>

clearly spells out his feeling of being foredoomed to impossible, but fructifying, infatuations:

> I could not love except where Death
> Was mingling his with Beauty's breath —
> Or Hymen, Time and Destiny
> Were stalking between her and me.

These couplets could very well be the motto of Poe's entire romantic life: his attraction to women doomed to die of
consumption; for safely married women; for women too old
to properly return his passion (the first Helen of his boyhood,
and, perhaps, even the wife of his adoptive guardian, Mr. Allan);
and for Sarah Helen Whitman.

In his story, "The Imp of the Perverse," Poe also defined
the impulse which drove him to his quixotic passions — yea,
to do the very thing that he knew would be the worst possible
course of action in a given situation. He wrote:

> a paradoxical something, which we may call
> perverseness, ... through its promptings we act without
> comprehensible object ... we act for the reason that we
> should not ... the assurance of the wrong or error of
> any action is often the one unconquerable force which
> impels us, and alone impels us, to its prosecution ...
> It is a radical, a primitive impulse — elementary ...
> The impulse increases to a wish, the wish to a desire,
> the desire to an uncontrollable longing, and the
> longing ... is indulged ... There is no passion in
> nature so demoniacally impatient, as that of him, who
> shuddering upon the edge of a precipice, thus
> meditates a plunge ... I am one of the many
> uncounted victims of the Imp of the Perverse.

<47>

About the Poems

I arranged the poems in this book to recreate the courtship, parting and remembrance of Helen and Poe. In the first section of the book, Poe's masterpiece "The Raven" is answered by Helen's valentine of the same title. Then each poet introduces characteristic poems, emphasizing their respective solitude.

Then, they demonstrate some of their best work to one another — both in love poems and in their verses on more far-ranging subjects. I chose poems they might have read to one another, pieces that would serve to deepen their mutual admiration.

Next come the poems associated with their parting, and the two poems that might have led to reconciliation — Helen's "Our Island of Dreams" and Poe's "Annabel Lee."

The remaining poems are Helen's posthumous tributes to Poe, and several additional Poe poems chosen for counterpoint. I believe this "dialogue" of poems shows both writers to their best advantage.

Among the fine later poems, Sarah Helen Whitman's "Proserpine, To Pluto, In Hades" deserves special attention for its personification of the characters in our drama. The poet uses the familiar mythical story of Ceres' daughter, Proserpine (Persephone in Greek), who must spend six months of the year with her brooding husband, Pluto, lord of the dead, and six months of the year above ground. This ancient fable explaining and symbolizing the seasons is turned topsy-turvy by Helen; she got the idea from her reading of Virgil. Her Proserpine *loves* Pluto and prefers to sit by his throne in the dark underworld. Her angry mother Ceres comes in a chariot drawn by two dragons to reclaim her. Here we have, a trio of archetypes: Helen, Poe and Helen's ever-angry mother. The Proserpine symbolism even carried to Helen's funeral in 1878: her coffin was decorated with a green wreath, and a stalk of wheat.

<48>

Helen's Romantic Masterpiece

Helen Whitman's longest and most ambitious poem is "Hours of Life." The middle section of that poem, "Noon," is included in this revised edition. It was excluded for reasons of space from the first printed edition. "Noon" is a spiritual saga and romantic quest — the poet's search for meaning and truth through the realms of myth and antiquity. In this long poetic odyssey we see: Echoes of Goethe in a passage that is almost a paraphrase of the famous scene of Faust alone in his laboratory, before he makes the acquaintance of Mephistopheles … A fascinatingly brief flirtation with the vengeful god of the Old Testament, whom she rejects … A wise examination and rejection of the sad religion of the Hindu … as well as the death-obsessed Egyptian … A passionate, almost Shelleyan plunge into the world of Ancient Greece, where she obviously feels close to the very origins of myth and meaning. Her use of the Dionysian Maenads — fierce, wild, drunken women, running down the mountain slope toward her as in a nightmare, crying out *"Evoe — ah — Evoe!"* is the most elemental, and frankly terrifying thing in all her writing. In fact, it is more Chthonic and *real* than many of the terrors in Poe's poetry.

She wrests herself away from the refrain of the Maenads only by turning to Nature. Here she waxes almost Byronic in taking comfort from the rude, natural world. She finds that she can accept this transcendental, all-encompassing Nature, free of the eidolons of ancient gods.

One thing only troubles her, though — the doubt that would bring her back to a more conventional, if still highly individual, resolution, in the third part of the poem. What about the abyss after death? she asks. Nature is *not* enough if the spirit does not survive and transcend the body. Thus she leaves her quest, Faust-like, with no satisfaction from all she has seen on her journey.

The beauty and power of "Noon" is easily obscured by the more conventional opening, and the rather spiritualist closing of the longer poem of which it is part. But "Noon" itself is a remarkable production, a piece Romantic in the purest sense. The very idea of a Providence widow in her darkened rooms

<49>

on Benefit Street writing such an impassioned, fully-worked out quest in verse is amazing. This poem has nothing much to do with Poe — but everything to do with why Poe must have been drawn to her.

Their Letters

I considered including the letters of Poe to Helen in this volume, but decided not to for several reasons. First, the letters have been reprinted and excerpted many times, and are readily available to readers. Second, while the poems seem to form a cohesive unity of encounter and reminiscence, and are markedly similar in style, no such colloquy could be created with Poe's and Mrs. Whitman's letters. Poe's letters to Helen are direct, passionate, immediate. Helen's letters to Poe have not survived. Instead, we have from her hand the cautious letters, written in latter years, to Poe's admirers and biographers.

In these missives, as befitting a lady writing to strangers, she is discreet, indirect, and highly formal. Poe's letters are conversational — we can hear the cadences of his voice in them. In no way can we believe that Sarah Helen Whitman spoke as she wrote in her many letters. The letters are valuable, indeed, and worth reading in John Carl Miller's exhaustive compilation of letters to John H. Ingram, *Poe's Helen Remembers* (University Press of Virginia, 1979.) Only in a dramatic, fictionalized form could we recreate the Helen whom Poe loved, and who attracted for many decades thereafter an inspired and admiring circle of loyal friends.

<50>

Helen's Providence

Sarah Helen Whitman lived in what is most kindly described as an intellectual backwater. Then, as now — and notwithstanding the presence of a major university — "native" Providence is a city mostly concerned with politics, formal religion, local history, and the outer trappings of culture. It is not a cosmopolitan city. As far as I can ascertain, Providence never had a literary silver age, let alone a golden one. It is a place that viewed visiting intellectuals with suspicion, and native ones with indifference, if not scorn. A number of gifted writers, male and female, have called Providence their home, but that did not mean they were welcome.

Sarah Helen sums up the dreariness of literary Providence thus in another letter to Ingram in 1874: "Though called the wealthiest city of its size in the Union, it has no magazine or other literary periodical."[1]

Helen's escapes to Boston and New York, her correspondence, and the intimate circle of her local admirers comprised her whole literary milieu. She emerged now and then as a "civic" poet, called upon to write an occasional piece for a dedication of a monument or graveyard, and then vanished into that most familiar state of poets — taken for granted. The editors of *Harper's* and other journals coaxed poems from her, which she pretended to submit with only the greatest reluctance. A poem such as her "Hours of Life" might have made the reputation of a young male poet.

She visited Emerson, and overcame her grave reservations to meet Walt Whitman when that controversial poet came to Providence. The former "lacked warmth," but the latter won her over by his integrity and eloquence. She confessed, however, that she had to tear out a full third of the pages from *Leaves of Grass* before she could keep the book in her house.

Even consenting to meet with Walt Whitman made Sarah Helen Whitman a member of Providence's *avant garde.* Years earlier, one of the most influential families in Providence broke off with Sarah Helen because she professed to have read and liked Percy Shelley. Anyone who even *read* the works of an

---

[1] SHW, letter of Feb 19, 1874, in *Poe's Helen Remembers*, p. 32

<51>

atheist could obviously be denied access to the proper kind of society in New England.

For some reason — perhaps a siege of requests by her friends and Poe's — Helen chose to publish a volume of her poems in 1853. Her decision was no doubt also influenced by her conviction that she would soon die. (She still had more than two hypochondriac decades left.)

Her first book, *Hours of Life and Other Poems*, published in her fiftieth year, was printed by Knowles, Anthony & Company under the aegis of George H. Whitney, a Providence bookseller and publisher. The edition was small and the poet was still giving away copies twenty years later. The book was produced and bound in boards with conventional blind embossing and a stamped spine. It is an undistinguished example of 1850s printing. The book does have ample margins and type in a legible size, and we can thank the printer and publisher for selecting durable rag paper instead of the new machine-made paper. Thanks to that choice, it is still possible to find copies of her book in good condition. The volume includes the major poems she had written to and about Poe.

We will never know if the bookseller published and underwrote *Hours of Life,* as Helen insisted, "at his request," or whether she subsidized the venture. We know that she wrote to Poe's biographer Ingram many years later: "I am utterly & entirely ignorant of all transactions with publishers. I have no relations with any publishers & never made a contract in my life." At another time, however, she wrote: "Mr. Whitney, the publisher, surrendered to me the copyright before he gave up business as bookseller and publisher. Mr. Carleton also gave up to me his copyright of *Edgar Poe and His Critics."*[1]

Edgar Poe and His Critics was published in 1860.

Sarah Helen Whitman's collected poems were issued in a memorial edition a year after her death, in 1879, by Houghton, Osgood and Company, printed by The Riverside Press, Cambridge, Massachusetts. The third and last printing was in 1916.

Sarah Helen Whitman had the prudence and foresight to leave a sum of $2,000 in her estate for the posthumous publication of her poems. No doubt this sum was applied to the 1879

---

[1] SHW, letter to Ingram, Feb 16, 1874, in *Poe's Helen Remembers,* pp. 29 & 97.

<52>

edition of her poems. The 1916 reprint, the same year as Caroline Ticknor's fine biography, (*Poe's Helen,* Charles Scribner's Sons, New York), was probably a spontaneous production.

When my limited first edition of this book was published in 1987, actors Norman George and Karen Lambert portrayed Poe and Helen in the Athenaeum as part of the publishing party, recreating the romance in a fine script written by Mr. George. Helen's voice was heard and read again for the first time in more than sixty years, in the very place where the romance blossomed.

Who Was Annabel Lee?

Sarah Helen remained convinced to the end of her days that "Annabel Lee" was Poe's remembrance and memorial to their romance. The dissimilarities of name, and Poe's breach with Sarah Helen, have inclined some biographers to dismiss this claim as vanity. After all, Poe's other great lady friend was *Annie* Richmond in Lowell, Massachusetts, and she is often proffered as the actual inspiration or object of the poem.

Was Helen deluded? She had her reasons:

First, the fact that the poem deals with a dead woman or a failed romance, makes it appropriate as a missive to Helen and entirely *in*appropriate to send to a present admirer. Even at his most morbid, Poe did not write to a lady of *her own* death, especially in that era of the "galloping consumption."

Helen insists that Poe varied and repeated a line from one of *her* poems in "Annabel Lee" — a sign that, if true, cannot be mistaken in intent. One of the secret pleasures of poets is to echo and transform something spoken by an "onlie begetter"— thus burying in a text for the world, a *secret* text for the eyes of the beloved only. Helen's earlier poem contains the line: *The night wind blew cold on my desolate heart.* Poe's "Annabel Lee" reads thus: *That the wind came out of the cloud by night.* Close, but not that convincing.

There are other, ample clues from the text of "Annabel Lee" itself. Poe writes "her high-born kinsmen came/ And bore her away from me ... our love it was stronger by far than

<53>

the love/ of those that were older than we — /Of many far wiser than we." Here, the high-born kinsmen and elders were those who opposed the marriage.

In additional correspondence that is reproduced in Caroline Ticknor's book, *Poe's Helen,* her biographer provided even more evidence to support Helen's story. As that book tells it:

> ...[D]uring the winter of 1849 she was suffering from chills and fever and her physician advised her to spend the winter with relatives in South Carolina; she decided that she would do so and planned to take a steamer from New York to Charleston. She wrote to Mrs. Osgood telling of this arrangement and asking her to meet her on board the boat, but at the last moment, the plan was relinquished and friends in New Bedford insisted that Mrs. Whitman should go to them; she therefore wrote to Mrs. Osgood that "just as she was about to seek the soft and balmy airs of the south some of her northern friends had 'caught her up' and 'borne her away' to the stern and rockbound shores of Massachusetts"... "Poe saw my letter to Mrs. Osgood," Mrs. Whitman states, "and referred to the words I used in the verse that has so puzzled the critics." "Of course," she concludes, "the filling up of the poem is in many ways purely imaginative. Yet every line and expression has a definite meaning when he speaks of 'a voice more familiar than his own'"[1]

In a statement of characteristic generosity, Helen adds, "Nevertheless I do not doubt that the poem may have had in his mind other shades of meaning and may have been in some way associated with other persons."[2] This statement is indicative of her essential fairness, an attitude not shared by the majority of women Poe knew. A gathering of the "true" Annabel Lees would have been interesting to behold!

Finally, the busy seaport Providence, although located at the head of a bay, *is* a "kingdom by the sea." Lowell, a mill town located inland on the Merrimack River, hardly qualifies.

---

[1] Ticknor, 130-31.
[2] *Ibid,* 131.

<54>

Helen recounts the other literary connection between the two poems thus in a letter to Ingram about her poem "Stanzas to Music," later re-titled "Our Island of Dreams:"

I will tell you their history, for it seems to imply a fatality — a prophetic instinct of the soul, apart from the conscious reason — something which overrules our voluntary actions & gives to them an unforeseen significance.

I had promised to furnish something for a new magazine to be called the American Metropolitan of which only two numbers were issued. Poe, who was engaged to write the literary notices for the periodical, wished me to send the "Lines to Arcturus" (written in October), & had himself carefully copied them for this purpose. After the rupture of our brief engagement, I withheld them, thinking their interior meaning might be apparent to many & give further notoriety to events whose publicity had already been sufficiently painful. Urged by the publisher to fulfill my promise for the February number, if only by sending half a dozen lines, & too ill, at the time, to write, I sought among my neglected manuscripts for something available, when I found three verses of an unfinished song, written four or five years before, for an Italian gentleman to accompany a wild, monotonous, dirge-like air which he had composed for the guitar. I had not seen them for years, but as I now read them, they sounded so strangely weird & mournful, so eloquent of all that I would have wished to express in reply to a letter which I had received from Edgar Poe soon after our final separation, a letter which I had not dared to answer, that I added the last verse & sent them without venturing to give myself time for reflection or hesitation. Of course they elicited a good deal of comment & conjecture, but I never regretted sending them. In his letter he [Poe] had urged me to write, if but one line, to assure him that I had not countenanced the cruel reports about the causes

<55>

which had led to our separation which had been so widely circulated. I had suffered so much through the opposition of my friends & family to the contemplated marriage that I dared not incur the repetition of the terrible scenes I had passed through by any direct communication with him.

I sent the stanzas to the publisher & they appeared in the February number, which I think was not issued until the middle of March, when the publisher failed & the magazine was discontinued. Meantime [Poe] had doubtless felt aggrieved & deeply wounded & had, perhaps, said & done some things which would, if known, place an inseparable gulf between us. After he had seen [my verses]... I believe that, knowing all earthly reconciliation between us impossible, he sought to express to me his undying love & remembrance in the most tender & spiritually imaginative of all his poems.

After that, no word ever passed between us, nor had I any indication from any source if his feeling toward me, until I heard of his death.

Yet I cannot doubt that he accepted my "Stanzas for Music" as a peace offering, nor can I doubt that in writing "Annabel Lee," the vague, sweet fantasy, so charming in its vagueness & obscurity, that he intended that I should read in it the veiled expression (visible to no eyes but mine) of his undying remembrance. . .
I think when you see in his letters the ingenuity & subtlety of his methods of conveying his thoughts without directly expressing them, you will understand my view of the subject & will not think it fanciful.[1]

Helen's poem titled "Song," with its telling lines "The fault was mine — mine only" was also published about this time.

There was an intended Poe-Helen "reunion" schemed by Poe's friends in Lowell. It failed when the two poets passed one another in opposing trains![2]

---

[1] SHW, letter to Ingram, Feb. 20, 1874, in *Poe's Helen Remembers*, pp. 35-6.
[2] SHW, letter to Ingram, Oct. 25, 1875, in *Poe's Helen Remembers*, p. 349

<56>

Her poem, "The Last Flowers," prophetic of Poe's death, was written in September, 1849, but it is doubtful that Helen found a way to convey it to Poe.

Poe's Estimation of Helen

Which of all her poems might Poe have read? "A Night in August," "Arcturus, Written in October" and "Our Island of Dreams" relate to Poe and were written while he was alive. Several stanzas of her poem, "The Raven," but not the longer poem in its final form, were conveyed to Poe after they were read in his honor at a Valentine's Day party in New York. Thus, Helen's "The Raven" *initiated* their romance in the winter of 1848.

We do not know which of her poems Poe read *before* they met in person. We do know that he spoke of her with mounting enthusiasm and praise even before her Valentine greeting. He read "Hours of Life" from Helen's manuscript and was astonished by it. It is important to recall that, in that era before typewriters and copiers, many editors and literati saw one another's works by passing around actual manuscript or other hand-written facsimiles. Poe certainly had seen some of her work in manuscript before, for he was able to recognize another of her anonymous poems merely from examining the handwriting.

Poe lectured in Lowell in the summer of 1848 and praised her poems. But the copy of the lecture that Poe later gave Griswold has only scant praise for her, calling her only one of the most *accomplished* female poets included in Griswold's collection. Helen points out correctly that the re-copied lecture was passed along during the period when she was no longer answering his letters and he had every emotional justification to erase a formerly-expressed high estimation.

> [In his Lowell lecture] he made a different estimate.
> He brought me the manuscript of the lecture and read
> me the portion extracted in Mr. Atkinson's notice. He
> said that he intended to *re*write the lecture when

<57>

Griswold's book on the female poets was out, & should then have very much more to say on the subject. But when his notice of Griswold's book came out in the Review, as copied into the "Literati," I saw only the cold & incidental allusion to my poems, which you may perhaps have seen there.

Elsewhere, Poe had privately expressed his opinion of Sarah Helen Whitman, even prior to their meeting, in a letter to Miss Anna Blackwell in June 1848:

Do you know Mrs. Whitman? I feel deep interest in her poetry and character. I have never seen her but once. Anne Lynch, however, told me many things about the romance of her character which singularly interested me and excited my curiosity. Her poet is, beyond question, *poetry* — instinct with genius. Can you not tell me something about her — anything — everything you know — and keep my secret — that is to say, let no one know that I have asked you to do so? May I trust you? I can — and will.

Helen says that Poe spoke of her as having "pre-eminence in refinement of art, enthusiasm, imagination & genius properly so called."[1] There is little reason to doubt the veracity of this attribution. In the light of the lies, slanders and exaggerations of the *literati,* Helen stands as almost the only one to place truth first. Various Poe admirers and biographers pressed her for information over the decades, and she gladly complied with reasonable and polite inquiries if they appeared to come from sincere admirers of Poe. She was many times piqued to see her disproof of some of the lurid anecdotes about Poe intentionally ignored. She loaned out many books, journals and ephemera, including some of her few actual specimens of Poe's handwriting. Many of these items were never returned to her.

As far as I can ascertain, she never exaggerated her relationship with Poe, and considered her major "mission" to be the defense of Poe's character — in order that his writing would survive to posterity. Though she had failed to "reform" him in

---

[1] Miller, *Poe's Helen Rememembers*, p. 66 fn.

<58>

life, she would do her best to defend him against the cruel accusations of his enemies.

Poe himself had not recovered from the shocks that had met him in Providence. He wrote a letter to the sympathetic Annie — who was *not* a poet, stating, "[F]rom this day forth I shun the pestilential society of *literary women.* They are a heartless, unnatural, venomous, dishonorable set, with no guiding principle but inordinate self-esteem." Poe did write letters of reconciliation to Helen, but he was convinced that her mother intercepted and destroyed them.

Lines Written to Arcturus

After Poe had won Helen's promise of marriage, and agreed to refrain absolutely from alcohol, he mentioned to her in parting some peculiarity about the star Arcturus — the fourth-brightest star in the heavens — which he wished her to observe. He may have asserted to her that Arcturus, although brighter than all the other stars in its constellation, was farther away. He later wrote back to Helen and said he was mistaken in this, and urged her to remove an astronomical footnote from the manuscript of her poem.

Both Poe and Helen appear to have been mistaken, at first, about the time of year in which Arcturus and its constellation Bootes can be viewed.

Helen herself relates how Arcturus intruded:

During the painful scenes which followed, I chanced to look toward the Western horizon & saw there *Arcturus* shining resplendently through a rift in the clouds, while *Ophiuchus,* or a star which I believed to be Ophiuchus, in the head of "the serpent," was faintly glimmering through the gathering darkness with a pale & sickly lustre.

To my excited imagination everything at that time seemed a portent or an omen. I had been subjected to terrible mental conflicts & was but imperfectly recovered from a painful & enervating illness.

<59>

That night, an hour after midnight, I wrote under a strange accession of prophetic exaltation the lines "To Arcturus," beginning "Star of resplendent front." The words from Virgil, *Nec morte esse locum,*" etc., were prefixed to them, though why I should then have thought them appropriate I cannot tell. I only remember that as I repeated the Latin words they had a sound so majestic, so exultant, so full of solemn & triumphant augury that the remembrance of it, even now, fills me with a mysterious joy … I had discovered soon after the lines were written that Arcturus & Ophiuchus must have been below the horizon when I thought I saw them thro' the western clouds & that it must have been some other stars I mistook for them.

When my poem was printed in my volume of poems it was therefore dated as if written in October.[1]

This careful recounting is indicative of Helen's attentiveness to detail, as well as her essential honesty. She wanted her correspondent to know that she had written a poem with portents of doom *early* in the romance and under the direct stimulation of remarks made by Poe. But then she hastened to explain her mistake in assuming that the first two stars that appeared in her window that night were the ones Poe had called to her attention, and notes that she amended the date on the poem to avoid an astronomical impossibility.

What Helen did not tell Ingram is that she moved the Virgil epigraph to the later "Arcturus" poem, where it is now found.

---

[1] SHW, letter to Ingram, March 16, 1874, in *Poe's Helen Remembers*, pp. 76-78.

<60>

Ulalume's Missing Stanza

The reader may be startled to see an "extra" stanza affixed to Poe's masterpiece "Ulalume" in this volume. Although Mabbot's edition of Poe's poems includes it, nearly all earlier editions do not contain the climactic stanza. Helen wrote to Ingram about this:

> I do not know whether you are acquainted with the last verse of "Ulalume" as originally printed. Poe omitted it at my suggestion, in a copy which he prepared for publication in the Providence *Journal*, with the above heading, & it is so printed in all the subsequent collections. He agreed with me that the penultimate verse made a more effective ending.

> Yesterday I went to the Providence Athenaeum Library & found the original version in the *American Whig Review*, edited by Colton. At the bottom of the page I found Poe's autograph, in pencil. It recalled to me a circumstance which I had entirely forgotten.

> "Ulalume" was published without signature & an anonymous copy had floated to me in some newspaper. I was strangely impressed with its weird imagery & vainly questioned everybody likely to have heard of it. One morning, being with Poe at the Athenaeum, I asked him if he had ever seen the poem & could tell me who wrote it. To my infinite surprise, he told me that he himself was the author. Turning to a bound volume of the *Review*, which was in the alcove where we were sitting, he wrote his name at the bottom, and I saw it again yesterday after an interval of more than 24 years.

Our edition includes the suppressed stanza, to restore it to the form in which Sarah Helen first read it and heard it from Poe's lips.

A further note about "Ulalume." I was startled to discover, upon reading Mabbott's edition of the complete poems, that this poem is taken by him, and hence, most readers, to represent a haunted *Halloween* night (October 31). From the evidence of the text itself, I heartily disagree. In the poem, the speaker

<61>

states that he "knew not the month was October." While this bereaved lover may indeed have lost track of his calendar, it is unlikely that one could pass though thirty-one days of October without knowing the month. It is far more likely *early* October, and the speaker has let the end of September slip by him in his distraction. "On this night of all nights in the year" is not Halloween, but the anniversary of the burial of Ulalume, "when I bore a dread burden down here." This poem is the Imp of the Perverse at work again, sending the poet to the worst place he can go at the worst possible time.

Poe also made a highly specific astronomical reference in "Ulalume." The star Astarte is the planet Venus, which on occasion forms an unforgettable triangle in the October sky: a crescent moon, the "double-horned crescent" of Venus (a detail only visible through a telescope), and the first-magnitude star Regulus in the constellation Leo. The poet is using the astronomical details precisely, and by using the mythological names of Astarte for Venus and "The Lion" for Leo, he invites all their mythological associations. Regulus (called *Cor Leonis* by the ancients) is a symbol of greatness and power, Venus of sensual love, and the moon — many things to many people. The poem may have baffled many readers, but that does not mean it lacks coherence and meaning.

Forgeries, Thefts, and Virginia Doris

As a pendant to the Poe inscription beneath "Ulalume," we must relate an ongoing controversy about the Athenaeum's Poe artifacts. When the *American Review* volume containing Poe's penciled-in name was displayed by the library in 1974, a Rhode Island Poe enthusiast named Virginia Doris sprang into action when she became convinced that the Poe "autograph" was a fake. She obtained professional opinions from a hand-writing expert and another Poe scholar that the inscription in the bound volume did not seem to be a Poe autograph. The slant of some letters was wrong, and Poe normally used a typographic (straight) letter "A" in his signature, not the rounded letter "A" found in the pencil inscription.

<62>

Sylvia Moubayed, Director of the Athenaeum at that time, attempted to determine whether the volume described by Mrs. Whitman might have been stolen in the intervening years. The bound volume of the journal containing Poe's poem was absolutely identical to the preceding and succeeding volumes in the series. There was no record of the volume ever having been lost, and no replacement volume was ever purchased or assembled for binding. As the Athenaeum did not have the resources to obtain a more professional evaluation of the "signature," the issue was left unresolved and Ms. Doris' assertions were gradually — but not intentionally — forgotten in the succeeding decades.

When I assembled the first edition of this book in the late 1980s, and when Jane Lancaster researched and wrote her history of the Providence Athenaeum in mid-2003, no present staff members of the library were aware of the quarter-century old controversy.

After the history, *Enquire Within: A Social History of the Providence Athenaeum,* was published, referring once again to the Poe autograph, an outraged Ms. Doris wrote furious letters to the Athenaeum and to local newspapers, demanding that the claim to possession of a Poe autograph be retracted. The Athenaeum was accused of having profited somehow from the "old wives' tale." Communications included a threat to take the matter to court.

When I finally looked at the pencil inscription for myself, I came to suspect that both Ms. Doris and the Athenaeum were right, and both were in error, and in different ways. First, it was a mistake for the library, Ms. Doris, and a handwriting expert to call the inscription an "autograph" and compare it to known autographs of Poe. The inscription is in pencil and was written hastily and in small script. If it is in Poe's hand it should only be compared to Poe's everyday handwriting, not to his formal autographs. As gentlemen do not write in library books, Poe's inscription was just emphatic enough to make the point of his authorship, but far short of an autograph.

The inscription has a leftward slant. Poe may have been standing while writing it, and the inscription is on a left-hand

<63>

page going toward the binding, an awkward spot in which to write, a position that would tend to make the writer slant the letters away from the binding.

I believe the fair question to resolve this matter is to ask, "Does this inscription bear a fair likeness to Poe's everyday handwriting?" Allowance also has to be made for the use of a pencil rather than a pen.

Here is the Poe inscription Helen found at the bottom of "Ulalume:"

The top of the lower case "d' in Edgar is almost not there; we have a rounded capital "A" and an upper case "P" less florid than Poe's usual style.

In examining Poe manuscripts photographically reproduced in several books about Poe, I see that Poe varied his writing between a simpler script and a highly calligraphic, almost typographic script. Although Poe came to favor a typographic, straight "A," such a letter is easier to make with a pen than a pencil. And, sure enough, I found the following example of Poe using a rounded capital "A" in the middle of his name:

The "P" in the pencil inscription is simpler than Poe's usual, more florid "P," but if the pencil was defective, as indicated from the broken "d," Poe may have opted for the easier capital "P ." Also bear in mind that Poe's lettering is scarcely larger than the type of the poem, so he was probably writing as he did when proofreading.

<64>

A definitive proof might come from comparing a similar pencil inscription known to be in Poe's hand, such as a marked-up typesetter's galley proof. Comparisons with Poe's more florid autographs, done in pen, are not appropriate.

It is not unreasonable, barring other evidence, that the *American Review* inscription is probably in Poe's hand, given that he was only writing his name to complete the printed text, not to add an autograph. So let us be fair on both sides by promising not to call it an autograph again.

When this issue was first raised by Ms. Doris in 1974, various theft and forgery scenarios were proffered. The original volume had been stolen or lost, it was suggested, and the Athenaeum quietly replaced it, with a librarian forging the inscription in his or her own hand. There is also the remote chance that an overzealous librarian *erased the inscription*, and then some other librarian faked the signature to undo the terrible mistake, and no one had been the wiser.

Mrs. Whitman's veracity about finding the inscription intact in the late 1870s cannot be doubted, and none of the directors of the Athenaeum had any motive to misrepresent the library's holdings. It is unfortunate that Ms. Doris' diligent research was forgotten by successive librarians, but I see no villains here, and no liars. No one has *profited* in any way from this matter — the Athenaeum would stand as a central locale in the Poe/Helen romance even if not one shred of paper remained to prove it. All parties are hereby invited to tea, or to a pow-wow at Sarah Helen Whitman's grave in the North Burial Ground, to bury the hatchet and share their mutual passion for Poe and Providence's Sarah Helen.[1]

Thanks to Jane Lancaster's fine work, we also now know that several full-sized, pen-and-ink autographs *were* in the Athenaeum all along. Poe checked out books during some of his visits, which required his signature on the host subscriber's account. Over the years since 1848, *all but one* of these autographs were carefully cut out with razor blades and secreted

---

[1] Virginia Doris died in 2007, and was buried in a conspicuous tomb in Swan Point cemetery, where "Poetess" is proudly inscribed beneath her name. Since her death no word, legal or spectral, has been heard from her regarding the Poe autograph.

<65>

out of the building. The Athenaeum now retains its last Poe autograph, dated December 21, 1848.

Helen Whitman's Beliefs

It is easy to look with a smile at the constellation of beliefs that made up "advanced" thinking in the 1850s to 1880s. On the surface, Sarah Helen Whitman belonged to the highly stratified, conventional world of a sensible, money-making seaport. With this came Christianity, stultifying sermons, and stern proscriptions against sensual indulgence.

At the same time, however, people read and spoke of things that were far afield from the narrow universe of the church steeple. The goods and new images of the East poured into Providence from the China Trade. Scholars began for the first time to compare the cultures and beliefs of East and West. Emerson looked East, and liked what he saw. Greek and Latin classics were there, and a large number of men and women could read for themselves of the glories of the ancient world — a world that mocked Puritanism.

Sarah Helen Whitman was certainly a well-read classicist. She knew Virgil, and her love of the classics even extended to appearing at least once in the robes and helmet of Athena. She read Shelley and the Romantics, and she translated German supernatural ballads, as well as Goethe, and Victor Hugo. Her many correspondents included Elizabeth Barrett Browning, Stephane Mallarmé and other continental writers, as well as domestic writers and editors.

Although some very "conventional" images and themes recur throughout her poems, it would be false to assume that Sarah Helen Whitman was just a social, political, theological and philosophical product of her time. She was an original, eccentric and Romantic. Had she been free of her duties of caring for her mother and sister — had she flown with Poe to New York City or even to Boston — there is little doubt that her originality would have blossomed or even exploded. What a loss to art when artists are trapped in family affairs!

<66>

While half the population was obsessed with industrialization and the accumulation of wealth, the New England avant garde, led by the transcendentalists, were opening new doors to the spiritual and supernatural. This bipolarity of practicality and dreaming makes American intellectual life fascinating. The same minds who fought for Darwin against the Bible, fought for Abolition against the profits of slavery as a Christian crusade," dabbled in spiritualism, and loved horror tales and Gothic poems.

Both poles are an enduring part of our heritage, and many of our most creative minds have contained a large dose of both tendencies. Providence's other great writer, H.P. Lovecraft, was the epitome of a materialist rationalist whose art consisted of a vast Mythos of dreams and nightmares. Walt Whitman understood this intellectual complexity when he wrote: "Do I contradict myself? Very well — I contradict myself. I am large — I contain multitudes."

Sarah Helen's dreaming side included a refined and individual brand of spiritualism. The first recorded séance in Providence took place in her parlor. Essentially, she nodded assent with the Christians on the issue of the immortality of the soul. But *her* afterlife is more pagan than Christian — a place where lovers are reunited, justice prevails, and punishment — that favorite bugaboo of Puritans — is not even mentioned. It is a benevolent vision of a "here and now" survival of souls — a comforting and harmless dream. She makes it clear in her poetry that she rejects the smiting God — the Old Testament Jehovah whose shadow still darkened New England.

Amidst the popular frenzy of séances and mediums, and their inevitable debunking and downfall, Helen clung to her belief in an afterlife, while dismissing with scorn the obvious charlatans who claimed to be able to converse with the dead. On one occasion she loaned some memento of Poe to a medium, but was not too surprised when the séance did not produce the hoped-for visitation.

Her studied attitude toward the supernatural is one that is in league with Poe's — a disbelief in death, essentially — and

<67>

almost identical with Lovecraft's a generation later. She summed it up thus: "I have a conviction not to be shaken that the occult sciences cover great truths, dimly discerned & obscured by superstition, doubtless, but nevertheless truths."

I would like to believe in Helen's spirits — but alas, I cannot. It would be nice to know that *she* is aware of this book — a belated offering on behalf of Poe to the woman he loved. That she loved *him,* the world may now judge how well.

Whitman endorsed a refined and individual brand of spiritualism. She attended the first recorded séance in Providence in September 1850, an event described as "not successful." Whitman did attend other séances, and contributed several highly intellectual letters and essays on the subject to the New York *Tribune* and to *The Spiritual Telegraph.* Their texts can be found in E.W. Capron's 1855 book *Modern Spiritualism*, and the author-enthusiast characterizes her thus: "Among the friends of the spiritual cause of Providence no one has exhibited more firmness, and none more readiness to defend in public and private the spiritual *theory* [emphasis mine] of these manifestations, than Mrs. Sarah Helen Whitman, the poetess. ... She always writes with vigor when reasoning on any subject, and does not forget to fortify herself with a strong array of facts" (234-235). Both Capron and Whitman seem eager to distance themselves from the Biblical spiritualism that seemed to come all too easy to fanatical Protestants. The metaphysics of 19th century spiritualism has many aspects that resemble latter-day "New Age" movements, including a startling tolerance for diversity of behavior (including a strong "free love" component.)

Although much has been made of Whitman's involvement with mediumship, I have come to suspect the veracity or accuracy of some of these claims. Richard P. Benton, for example, describes Whitman as already involved in séances at the time of her romance with Poe, wearing a wooden coffin around her neck as a *memento mori.* This somewhat trivializes and ridicules her — in 1848, no séance had as yet occurred in Providence, and in fact the Spiritualist movement was then just starting in upstate New York.

<68>

Spiritualists like to claim Whitman as a celebrity member of their movement, but I find scant evidence of her participation in it on more than a local, social level. Her recognition in the field is from her occasional correspondence and journalism; I was not able to find her name anywhere among officers or attendees at various spiritualist conventions held in the Northeast. It is also significant that she makes no claims of mediumship in her poetry, nor in her correspondence with Poe's biographer Ingram. (In her letters to Ingram, she several times alludes to certain beliefs about things spiritual, but she refrains from offering them. She also hints that the "truths" she had come to accept had come to her unbidden.) Not one syllable of her work is "dictated" by spirits. Except in the parody poem, "The Raven," Whitman in fact never imitates Poe in style, and her influences are British and Classical through and through. A few possessed women poets did write "channeled" poems from Poe, and they are as awful as one might expect; Mrs. Whitman was not one of their number.

More needs to be learned about Mrs. Whitman's involvement, in prose, in the antislavery and suffrage movements. Although I located her poem, "Lines Written in November," and another, "The Golden Ball," in *Liberty Chimes*, an antislavery journal, neither poem could be construed as expressive, or symbolic, of political struggle. Her inclusion there implies her support of the cause, and little else.

Brett Rutherford
December 1986/ July 2003/March 2008/
November 2011
Providence, Rhode Island

P.S. This fourth edition provided an opportunity to add, at the suggestion of a reader and correspondent, Bill Hahn, Mrs. Whitman's brief "Stanzas" addressed to Poe in reply to his sending of "To Helen." I also added Mrs. Whitman's 1876 translation of Stephane Mallarmé's poem on "The Tomb of Edgar Poe." A number of minor line break and punctuation errors have been addressed, and some footnotes added. All unattributed footnotes are mine; Mrs. Whitman's are marked "SHW."

<69>

BIBLIOGRAPHY

Austin, John O. "One Line of the Power Family." *Narragansett Historical Register.* January, 1889. pp. 17-23. [Monograph of the same title at Rhode Island Historical Society Library genealogy collection is actually a reprint of this article.]

Benton, Richard P. "Friends and Enemies: Women in the Life of Edgar Allan Poe" in *Myths and Reality.* 1987. Baltimore: The Edgar Allan Poe Society.

Capron, E.W. *Modern Spiritualism: Its Facts and Fanaticisms, Its Consistencies and Contradictions.* 1855. Boston: Bela Marsh.

Conrad, Susan P. *Perish the Thought: Intellectual Women in Romantic America 1830-1860.* 1976. New York: Oxford Univ. Press.

Lancaster, Jane. *Inquire Within: A Social History of the Providence Athenaeum Since 1753.* 2003. Providence: The Providence Athenaeum.

Miller, John Carl, ed. *Poe's Helen Remembers.* 1979. Charlottesville, VA: University Press of Virginia.

Poe, Edgar Allan. *Complete Poems.* Thomas Ollive Mabbott, ed. (1968). 2000. Urbana, IL: University of Illinois Press.

Powers, Franklin E. *A genealogical record of the Powers(s) Families.* 1974. Aurora, Colorado: Powers. At Rhode Island Historical Society Library Genealogy Collection.

Quinn, Arthur Hobson. *Edgar Allan Poe: A Critical Biography.* 1941. New York: D. Appleton-Century Co.

Richards, Eliza. "Lyric Telegraphy: Women Poets, Spiritualist Poetics, and the 'Phantom Voice' of Poe." *Yale Journal of Criticism,* Vol. 12 No. 2. 1999. pp. 269-294.

Silverman, Kenneth. *Edgar A. Poe: Mournful and Never-Ending Remembrance.* 1991. New York: HarperCollins Publishers.

Thomas, Dwight, and David K. Jackson. *The Poe Log: A Documentary Life of Edgar Allan Poe 1809-1849.* 1987. New York: G.K. Hall & Co.

Ticknor, Caroline. *Poe's Helen.* 1916. New York. Charles Scribner's Sons.

Whitman, Sarah Helen. *Hours of Life, And Other Poems.* 1853. Providence: George H, Whitney.

———. "Lines Written in November." *Liberty Chimes.* 1845: Providence: Providence Ladies' Antislavery Society.

———. *Poems.* 1879. Boston: Houghton, Osgood and Company.

———.. "To Edgar Allan Poe [The Raven]" *Home Journal.* March 18, 1848.

<70>

LAST FLOWERS

The poems by Edgar Allan Poe
are identified with the image
of the RAVEN.

The poems by Sarah Helen Whitman
are identified with the image
of the DOVE.

THE RAVEN

Once upon a midnight dreary,
 while I pondered, weak and weary,
Over many a quaint and curious
 volume of forgotten lore —
While I nodded, nearly napping,
 suddenly there came a tapping,
As of someone gently rapping,
 rapping at my chamber door —
"'Tis some visitor," I muttered,
 "tapping at my chamber door —
Only this and nothing more."

Ah, distinctly I remember
 it was in the bleak December;
And each separate dying ember
 wrought its ghost upon the floor.
Eagerly I wished the morrow; —
 vainly had I sought to borrow
From my books surcease of sorrow —
 sorrow for the lost Lenore —
For the rare and radiant maiden
 whom the angels name Lenore —
Nameless *here* for evermore.

<73>

And the silken, sad, uncertain rustling
    of each purple curtain
Thrilled me — filled me with fantastic
    terrors never felt before;
So that now, to still the beating of
    my heart, I stood repeating
"'Tis is some visitor entreating entrance
    at my chamber door —
Some late visitor entreating entrance at
    my chamber door; —
    This it is and nothing more."

Presently my soul grew stronger;
    hesitating then no longer,
"Sir," said I, "or Madam, truly,
    your forgiveness I implore;
But the fact is I was napping,
    and so gently you came rapping,
And so faintly you came tapping,
    tapping at my chamber door,
That I scarce was sure I heard you"—
    here I opened wide the door; —-
    Darkness there and nothing more.

<74>

Deep into that darkness peering,
　　long I stood there wondering, fearing,
Doubting, dreaming dreams no mortal
　　ever dared to dream before;
But the silence was unbroken,
　　and the stillness gave no token,
And the only word there spoken
　　was the whispered word, "Lenore?"
This I whispered, and an echo murmured
　　back the word, "Lenore"
　Merely this and nothing more.

Back into the chamber turning,
　　all my soul within me burning,
Soon again I heard a tapping
　　somewhat louder than before.
"Surely," said I, "surely that is something
　　at my window lattice;
Let me see, then, what thereat is,
　　and this mystery explore —
Let my heart be still a moment
　　and this mystery explore; —
　'Tis the wind and nothing more!"

<76>

Open here I flung the shutter,
    when, with many a flirt and flutter,
In there stepped a stately Raven
    of the saintly days of yore;
Not the least obeisance made he;
    not a minute stopped or stayed he;
But, with mien of lord or lady,
    perched above my chamber door —
Perched upon a bust of Pallas
    just above my chamber door —
  Perched, and sat, and nothing more.

Then this ebony bird beguiling
    my sad fancy into smiling,
By the grave and stern decorum
    of the countenance it wore,
"Though thy crest be shorn or shaven,
    thou," I said, "art sure no craven,
Ghastly grim and ancient Raven
    wandering from the Nightly shore —
Tell me what thy lordly name is
    on the Night's Plutonian shore!"
  Quoth the Raven "Nevermore."

<77>

Much I marveled this ungainly
    fowl to hear discourse so plainly,
Though its answer little meaning —
    little relevancy bore;
For we cannot help agreeing
    that no living human being
Ever yet was blessed with seeing bird
    above his chamber door —
Bird or beast upon the sculptured
    bust above his chamber door,
  With such name as "Nevermore."

But the Raven, sitting lonely
    on the placid bust, spoke only
That one word, as if his soul in that
    one word he did outpour.
Nothing farther then he uttered —
    not a feather then he fluttered —
Till I scarcely more than muttered
    "Other friends have flown before —
On the morrow *he* will leave me,
    as my Hopes have flown before."
  Then the bird said "Nevermore."

<78>

Startled at the stillness broken
     by reply so aptly spoken,
"Doubtless," said I, "what it utters
     is its only stock and store
Caught from some unhappy master
     whom unmerciful Disaster
Followed fast and followed faster
     till his songs one burden bore —
Till the dirges of his Hope that
     melancholy burden bore
  Of 'Never — nevermore.'"

But the Raven still beguiling
     my sad fancy into smiling,
Straight I wheeled a cushioned seat
     in front of bird, and bust and door;
Then, upon the velvet sinking,
     I betook myself to linking
Fancy unto fancy, thinking
     what this ominous bird of yore —
What this grim, ungainly, ghastly,
     gaunt and ominous bird of yore
  Meant in croaking "Nevermore."

< 79 >

This I sat engaged in guessing,
  but no syllable expressing
To the fowl whose fiery eyes
  now burned into my bosom's core;
This and more I sat divining,
  with my head at ease reclining
On the cushion's velvet lining
  that the lamplight gloated o'er,
But whose velvet-violet lining
  with the lamp-light gloating o'er,
  She shall press, ah, nevermore!

Then, methought, the air grew denser,
  perfumed from an unseen censer
Swung by seraphim whose footfalls
  tinkled on the tufted floor.
"Wretch," I cried, "thy God hath lent thee —
  by these angels he hath sent thee
Respite — respite and nepenthe
  from thy memories of Lenore;
Quaff, oh quaff this kind nepenthe
  and forget this lost Lenore!"
  Quoth the Raven "Nevermore."

<80>

"Prophet" said I, "thing of evil! —
  prophet still, if bird or devil! —
Whether Tempter sent, or whether
  tempest tossed thee here ashore,
Desolate yet all undaunted,
  on this desert land enchanted —
On this home by Horror haunted —
  tell me truly, I implore —
Is there — *Is* there balm in Gilead? —
  tell me — tell me, I implore!"
  Quoth the Raven "Nevermore."

"Prophet!" said I, "thing of evil! —
  prophet still, if bird or devil!
By that Heaven that bends above us —
  by that God we both adore —
Tell this soul with sorrow laden
  if, within the distant Aidenn,
It shall clasp a sainted maiden
  whom the angels name Lenore —
Clasp a rare and radiant maiden
  whom the angels name Lenore."
  Quoth the Raven "Nevermore."

"Be that word our sign of parting,
   bird or fiend!" I shrieked, upstarting —
"Get thee back into the tempest
   and the Night's Plutonian shore!
Leave no black plume as a token
   of that lie thy soul hath spoken!
Leave my loneliness unbroken! —
   quit the bust above my door!
Take thy beak from out my heart,
   and take thy form from off my door!"
   Quoth the Raven "Nevermore."

And the Raven, never flitting,
   still is sitting, *still* is sitting
On the pallid bust of Pallas
   just above my chamber door;
And his eyes have all the seeming
   of a demon's that is dreaming,
And the lamp-light o'er him streaming
   throws his shadow on the floor;
And my soul from out that shadow
   that lies floating on the floor
Shall be lifted — nevermore!

1844-1849

<82>

TO E.A. POE

A Valentine, February 1848

A Raven true as ever flapped
    his heavy wing
against the window of the sick
    and croaked "Despair."
— Young's "Revenge"

Oh! thou grim and ancient Raven,
From the Night's Plutonic shore,
Oft in dreams, thy ghastly pinions
Wave and flutter round my door —
Oft thy shadow dims the moonlight
Sleeping on my chamber floor.

Romeo talks of "White dove trooping,[1]
Amid crows athwart the night:"
But to see thy dark wing swooping
Down the silvery path of light,
Amid swans and dovelets stooping,
Were to me, a nobler sight.

Oft amid the twilight glooming
Round some grim ancestral tower
In the lurid distance looming,
I can see thy pinions lower, —
Hear thy sullen storm-cry booming
Thro' the lonely midnight hour.

---

[1] *White dove trooping. Romeo and Juliet*, I.v.

<83>

Oft this work-day world forgetting,
From its toil curtain'd snug,
By the sparkling embers sitting
On the richly broidered rug,
Something round about me flitting
Glimmers like a "Golden Bug."

Dreamily its path I follow,
In a "bee line" to the moon
Till, into some dreamy hollow
Of the midnight sinking soon,
Lo! he glides away before me
And I lose the golden boon.

Oft like Proserpine I wander
On the Night's Plutonic shore,
Hoping, fearing, while I ponder
On thy loved and lost Lenore,
Till thy voice like distant thunder
Sounds across the distant moor.

From thy wing, one purple feather
Wafted o'er my chamber floor
Like a shadow o'er the heather,
Charms my vagrant fancy more
Than all the flowers I used to gather
On "Idalia's velvet shore."[1]

---

[1] *Idalia's velvet shore.* An allusion to Thomas Gray's "The Progress of
Poesy, I.3, line 3.

<84>

Then, Oh! Grim and Ghastly Raven!
Wilt thou to my heart and ear
Be a Raven true as ever
Flapped his wings and croaked "Despair"?
Not a bird that roams the forest
Shall our lofty eyrie share.

— *Providence, R.I., February 14, 1848*

<85>

THE RAVEN

Raven, from the dim dominions
On the Night's Plutonian shore,
Oft I hear thy dusky pinions
Wave and flutter round my door —
See the shadow of thy pinions
Float along the moon-lit floor;

Often, from the oak-woods glooming
Round some dim ancestral tower,
In the lurid distance looming —
Some high solitary tower —
I can hear thy storm-cry booming
Through the lonely midnight hour.

When the moon is at the zenith,
Thou dost haunt the moated hall,
Where the marish flower greeneth
O'er the waters, like a pall —
Where the House of Usher leaneth,
Darkly nodding to its fall:

There I see thee, dimly gliding —
See thy black plumes waving slow —
In its hollow casements hiding,
When their shadow yawns below,
To the sullen tarn confiding
The dark secrets of their woe: —

<86>

See thee, when the stars are burning
	In their cressets, silver clear —
When Ligeia's spirit yearning
	For the earth-life, wanders near —
When Morella's soul returning,
	Weirdly whispers "I am here."

Once, within a realm enchanted,
	On a far isle of the seas,
By unearthly visions haunted,
	By unearthly melodies,
Where the evening sunlight slanted
	Golden through the garden trees —

Where the dreamy moonlight dozes,
	Where the early violets dwell,
Listening to the silver closes
	Of a lyric loved too well,
Suddenly, among the roses,
	Like a cloud, thy shadow fell.

Once, where Ulalume lies sleeping,
	Hard by Auber's haunted mere,
With the ghouls a vigil keeping,
	On that night of all the year,
Came thy sounding pinions, sweeping
	Through the leafless woods of Weir!

<87>

Oft, with Proserpine I wander
   On the Night's Plutonian shore,
Hoping, fearing, while I ponder
   On thy loved and lost Lenore —
On the demon doubts that sunder
   Soul from soul forevermore;
Trusting, though with sorrow laden,
   That when life's dark dream is o'er,
By whatever name the maiden
   Lives within thy mystic lore,
Eiros, in that distant Aidenn,
   Shall his Charmion meet once more.

<88>

TO HELEN

Helen, thy beauty is to me
   Like those Nicean barks of yore,
That gently, o'er a perfumed sea,
   The weary, way-worn wanderer bore
   To his own native shore.

On desperate seas long wont to roam,
   Thy hyacinth hair, thy classic face,
Thy Naiad airs have brought me home
   To the glory that was Greece,
And the grandeur that was Rome.

Lo! in yon brilliant window-niche
   How statue-like I see thee stand,
The agate lamp within thy hand!
   Ah, Psyche, from the regions which
  Are Holy-Land!

1831-1843

<89>

TO HELEN

I saw thee once — once only —
     years ago:
I must not say *how* many — but
     not many.
It was a July midnight; and from out
A full-orbed moon, that, like thine own soul, soaring,
Sought a precipitate pathway up through heaven,
There fell a silvery-silken veil of light,
With quietude, and sultriness, and slumber,
Upon the upturned faces of a thousand
Roses that grew in an enchanted garden,
Where no wind dared to stir, unless on tiptoe —
Fell on the upturn'd faces of those roses
That gave out, in return for the love-light,
Their odorous souls in an ecstatic death —
Fell on the upturned faces of these roses
That smiled and died in this parterre, enchanted
By thee, and by the poetry of thy presence.

Clad all in white, upon a violet bank
I saw thee half-reclining; while the moon
Fell on the upturned faces of the roses,
And on thine own, upturn'd — alas, in sorrow!

Was it not Fate, that, on this July midnight —
Was it not Fate, (whose name is also Sorrow,)
That bade me pause before that garden-gate,
To breathe the incense of those slumbering roses?

<91>

No footstep stirred: the hated world all slept,
Save only thee and me. (Oh, Heaven! — oh, God!
How my heart beats at coupling those two words!)
Save only thee and me. I paused — I looked —
And in an instant all things disappeared.
(Ah, bear in mind this garden was enchanted!)
The pearly lustre of the moon went out:
The mossy banks and the meandering paths,
The happy flowers and the repining trees,
Were seen no more: the very roses' odors
Died in the arms of the adoring airs.
All — all expired save thee — save less than thou:
Save only the divine light in thine eyes —
Save but the soul in thine uplifted eyes.
I saw but them — they were the world to me!
I saw but them — saw only them for hours,
Saw only them until the moon went down.
What wild heart-histories seemed to lie enwritten
Upon those crystalline, celestial spheres!
How dark a woe, yet how sublime a hope!
How silently serene a sea of pride!
How daring an ambition! yet how deep —
How fathomless a capacity for love!

But now, at length, dear Dian sank from sight,
Into a western couch of thunder-cloud;
And thou, a ghost, amid the entombing trees
Didst glide away. *Only thine eyes remained;*
They *would not* go — they never yet have gone;
Lighting my lonely pathway home that night,
They have not left me (as my hopes have) since;

<92>

They follow me — they lead me through the years.
They are my ministers — yet I their slave.
Their office is to illumine and enkindle —
My duty, *to be saved* by their bright light,
And purified in their electric fire,
And sanctified in their elysian fire.
They fill my soul with Beauty (which is Hope,)
And are far up in Heaven — the stars I kneel to
In the sad, silent watches of my night;
While even in the meridian glare of day
I see them still—two sweetly scintillant
Venuses, unextinguished by the sun!

1848-1849

<93>

STANZAS

A low and bewildering melody
Is murmuring in my ear —
Tones such as in the twilight wood
The aspen thrills to hear
When Faunus slumbers on the hill
and all entranced boughs are still.

The jasmine twines her snowy stars
Into a fairer wreath —
The lily through my lattices bars
Exhales a sweeter breath —
And, gazing on night's starry cope,
I dwell with "Beauty which is Hope."

August 1848

<94>

THE PAST

So fern, und doch so nah.—GOETHE.

Thick darkness broodeth o'er the world:
  The raven pinions of the Night,
Close on her silent bosom furled,
  Reflect no gleam of orient light.
E'en the wild Norland fires[1] that mocked
  The faint bloom of the eastern sky,
Now leave me, in close darkness locked,
  Tonight's weird realm of fantasy.

Borne from pale shadow-lands remote,
  A morphean music, wildly sweet,
Seems, on the starless gloom, to float,
  Like the white-pinioned Paraclete.
Softly into my dream it flows,
  Then faints into the silence drear;
While from the hollow dark outgrows
  The phantom Past, pale gliding near.

The visioned Past; so strangely fair!
  So veiled in shadowy, soft regrets.
So steeped in sadness, like the air
  That lingers when the day-star sets!
Ah! could I fold it to my heart,
  On its cold lips my kisses press,
This waste of aching life impart,
  To win it back from nothingness!

---

[1] *Norland fires.* The Northern Lights, or Aurora Borealis. New
England experienced intense displays of the Northern Lights in the
years 1835 to 1860.

<95>

I loathe the purple light of day,
    And shun the morning's golden star,
Beside that shadowy form to stray,
    Forever near, yet oh how far!
Thin as a cloud of summer even,
    All beauty from my gaze it bars;
Shuts out the silver cope of heaven,
    And glooms athwart the dying stars.

Cold, sad, and spectral, by my side,
    It breathes of love's ethereal bloom —
Of bridal memories, long affied
    To the dread silence of the tomb:
Sweet, cloistered memories, that the heart
    Shuts close within its chalice cold;
Faint perfumes, that no more dispart
    From the bruised lily's floral fold.

"My soul is weary of her life;"[1]
    My heart sinks with a slow despair;
The solemn, star-lit hours are rife
    With fantasy; the noontide glare,
And the cool morning, fancy free,
    Are false with shadows; for the day
Brings no blithe sense of verity,
    Nor wins from twilight thoughts away.

---

[1] *My soul is weary of her life.* Job 10:1.

<96>

Oh, bathe me in the Lethean stream,
   And feed me on the lotus flowers;
Shut out this false, bewildering dream,
   This memory of departed hours!
Sweet haunting dream! so strangely fair —
   So veiled in shadowy, soft regrets —
So steeped in sadness, like the air
   That lingers when the day-star sets!

The Future can no charm confer,
   My heart's deep solitudes to break;
No angel's foot again shall stir
   The waters of that silent lake.
I wander in pale dreams away,
   And shun the morning's golden star,
To follow still that failing ray,
   Forever near, yet oh how far!

February 1846

<97>

ULALUME

The skies they were ashen and sober;
   The leaves, they were
       crispèd and sere —
   The leaves, they were withering and sere:
It was night, in the lonesome October
   Of my most immemorial year;
It was hard by the dim lake of Auber,
   In the misty mid region of Weir: —
It was down by the dank tarn of Auber,
   In the ghoul-haunted woodland of Weir.

Here once, through an alley Titanic,
   Of cypress, I roamed with my Soul —
   Of cypress, with Psyche, my Soul.
These were days when my heart was volcanic
   As the scoriac rivers that roll —
   As the lavas that restlessly roll
Their sulphurous currents down Yaanek
   In the ultimate climes of the Pole —
That groan as they roll down Mount Yaanek
   In the realms of the Boreal Pole.

Our talk had been serious and sober,
   But our thoughts they were palsied and sere —
   Our memories were treacherous and sere —
For we knew not the month was October,
   And we marked not the night of the year —
   (Ah, night of all nights in the year!)
We noted not the dim lake of Auber —
   (Though once we had journeyed down here)
We remembered not the dank tarn of Auber,
   Nor the ghoul-haunted woodland of Weir.

<98>

And now, as the night was senescent,
    And star-dials pointed to morn —
    As the star-dials hinted of morn —
At the end of our path a liquescent
    And nebulous lustre was born,
Out of which a miraculous crescent
    Arose with a duplicate horn —
Astarte's bediamonded crescent
    Distinct with its duplicate horn.

And I said — "She is warmer than Dian;
    She rolls through an ether of sighs —
    She revels in a region of sighs.
She has seen that the tears are not dry on
    These cheeks where the worm never dies,
And has come past the stars of the Lion,
    To point us the path to the skies —
    To the Lethean peace of the skies —
Come up, in despite of the Lion,
    To shine on us with her bright eyes —
Come up through the lair of the Lion,
    With love in her luminous eyes."

But Psyche, uplifting her finger,
    Said, "Sadly this star I mistrust —
    Her pallor I strangely mistrust —
Oh, hasten! — oh, let us not linger!
    Oh, fly! — let us fly! — for we must."
In terror she spoke, letting sink her
    Wings till they trailed in the dust —
In agony sobbed, letting sink her
    Plumes till they trailed in the dust —
    Till they sorrowfully trailed in the dust.

<99>

I replied — "This is nothing but dreaming.
Let us on, by this tremulous light!
Let us bathe in this crystalline light!
Its Sybillic splendor is beaming
With Hope and in Beauty tonight —
See! — it flickers up the sky through the night!
Ah, we may safely trust to its gleaming
And be sure it will lead us aright —
We surely may trust to a gleaming
That cannot but guide us aright
Since it flickers up to Heaven through the night."

Thus I pacified Psyche and kissed her,
And tempted her out of her gloom —
And conquered her scruples and gloom;
And we passed to the end of the vista,
But were stopped by the door of a tomb —
By the door of a legended tomb;
And I said — "What is written, sweet sister,
On the door of this legended tomb?"
She replied — "Ulalume — Ulalume —
'T is the vault of thy lost Ulalume!"
Then my heart it grew ashen and sober
As the leaves that were crispèd and sere —
As the leaves that were withering and sere;
And I cried — "It was surely October
On *this* very night of last year
That I journeyed — I journeyed down here! —
That I brought a dread burden down here —
On this night, of all nights in the year,
Ah, what demon has tempted me here?

<100>

Well I know, now, this dim lake of Auber —
    This misty mid region of Weir —
Well I know, now, this dank tarn of Auber,
    This ghoul-haunted woodland of Weir."

Said we, then — the two, then —
    "Ah, can it Have been that
        the woodlandish ghouls —
    The pitiful, the merciful ghouls,
To bar up our way and to ban it
    From the secret that lies in these wolds —
    From the thing that lies hidden in these wolds —
Have drawn up the spectre of a planet
    From the limbo of lunary souls —
This sinfully scintillant planet
    From the Hell of the planetary souls?"

1847-1849

<101>

ARCTURUS

Written in October
"Our star looks through the storm."

Star of resplendent front!
    thy glorious eye
Shines on me still from out yon clouded sky —
Shines on me through the horrors of a night
More drear than ever fell o'er day so bright —
Shines till the envious Serpent slinks away,
And pales and trembles at thy steadfast ray.

Hast thou not stooped from Heaven, fair star? to be
So near me in this hour of agony? —
So near — so bright — so glorious, that I seem
To lie entranced as in some wondrous dream —
All earthly joys forgot—all earthly fear,
Purged in the light of thy resplendent sphere:
Kindling within my soul a pure desire
To blend with thine its incandescent fire —
To lose my very life in thine, and be
Soul of thy soul through all eternity.

<102>

LINES WRITTEN IN NOVEMBER

Farewell the forest shade,
the twilight grove,
The turfy path with fern and flowers inwove,
Where through long summer days I wandered far,
Till warned of Evening by her folding star.
No more I linger by the fountain's play,
Where arching boughs shut out the sultry ray,
Making at noontide hours a dewy gloom
O'er the moist marge, where weeds and
wild flowers bloom;
Till, from the western sun, a glancing flood
Of arrowy radiance filled the twilight wood,
Glinting athwart each leafy, verdant fold,
And flecking all the turf with drops of gold.

Sweet sang the wild bird on the waving bough
Where cold November winds are wailing now;
The chirp of insects on the sunny lea,
And the low, drowsy bugle of the bee,
Are silent all; closed is their vesper lay,
Borne by the breeze of Autumn far away.
Yet still the withered heath I love to rove,
The bare, brown meadow, and the leafless grove;
Still love to tread the bleak hill's rocky side,
Where nodding asters wave in purple pride,
Or, from its summit, listen to the flow
Of the dark waters, booming far below.
Still through the tangling, pathless copse I stray,
Where sere and rustling leaves obstruct the way,
To find the last, pale blossom of the year,

<103>

That strangely blooms when all is dark and drear;
The wild witch-hazel, fraught with mystic power
To ban or bless, as sorcery rules the hour.
Then, homeward wending, through the dusky vale,
Where winding rills their evening damps exhale,
Pause by the dark pool, in whose sleeping wave
Pale Dian loves her golden locks to lave;
As when she stole upon Endymion's rest,
And his young dreams with heavenly beauty blest.
And thou, "stern ruler of the inverted year,"[1]
Cold, cheerless Winter, hath thy wild career
No sweet, peculiar pleasures for the heart,
That can ideal worth to rudest forms impart?
When, through thy long, dark nights,
      cold sleet and rain
Patter and plash against the frosty pane,
Warm curtained from the storm, I love to lie,
Wakeful, and listening to the lullaby
Of fitful winds, that as they rise and fall
Send hollow murmurs through the echoing hall.
  Oft, by the blazing hearth at even-tide,
I love to see the fitful shadows glide,
In flickering motion, o'er the illumined wall,
Till slumber's honey-dew my senses thrall;
Then, while in dreamy consciousness, I lie
'Twixt sleep and waking, fairy fantasy
Culls, from the golden past, a treasured store,
And weaves a dream so sweet, hope could
      not ask for more.

---

[1] *Stern ruler of the inverted year.* From the "Winter" section of Thomson's *The Seasons.*

<104>

In the cold splendor of a frosty night,
When blazing stars burn with intenser light
Through the blue vault of heaven;
      when the keen air
Sculptures in bolder lines the uplands bare;
When sleeps the shrouded earth, in solemn trance,
Beneath the wan moon's melancholy glance;
I love to mark earth's sister planets rise,
And in pale beauty tread the midnight skies;
Where, like lone pilgrims, constant as the night,
They fill their dark urns from the fount of light.
      I love the Borealis flames that fly,
Fitful and wild, athwart the northern sky;
The storied constellations, like a page
Fraught with the wonders of a former age,
Where monsters grim, Gorgons and Hydras rise,
And "gods and heroes blaze along the skies."[1]
      Thus Nature's music, various as the hour,
Solemn or sweet, hath ever mystic power
Still to preserve the unperverted heart
Awake to love and beauty; to impart
Treasures of thought and feeling, pure and deep,
That aid the doubting soul
      its heavenward course to keep.

c. 1845

---

[1] *Gods and heroes blaze along the skies.* From William Hamilton Drummond. *The Giant's Causeway* (1811): "Lions and Centaurs, Gorgons, Hydras, rise,/ And gods and heroes blaze along the skies."

<105>

ISRAFEL

And the angel Israfel, whose heart-
strings are a lute,
and who has the sweetest voice of all
God's creatures—Koran

In Heaven a spirit doth dwell
    "Whose heart-strings are a lute;"
None sing to wildly well
As the angel Israfel,
And the giddy Stars (so legends tell)
Ceasing their hymns, attend the spell
    Of his voice, all mute.

Tottering above
    In her highest noon,
    The enamoured moon
Blushes with love,
    While, to listen, the red levin
    (With the rapid Pleiads, even,
    Which were seven,)
    Pauses in Heaven.

And they say (the starry choir
    And the other listening things)
That Israfel's fire
Is owing to that lyre
    By which he sits and sings —
The trembling living wire
    Of those unusual strings.

<106>

But the skies that angel trod,
    Where deep thoughts are a duty —
Where Love's a grown-up God —
    Where the Houri glances are
Imbued with all the beauty
    Which we worship in a star.

Therefore thou art not wrong,
    Israfeli, who despisest
An unimpassioned song;
To thee the laurels belong,
    Best bard, because the wisest!
Merrily live, and long!

The ecstasies above
    With thy burning measures suit —
Thy grief, thy joy, thy hate, thy love,
    With the fervour of thy lute —
    Well may the stars be mute!

Yes, Heaven is thine; but this
    Is a world of sweets and sours;
    Our flowers are merely — flowers,
And the shadow of thy perfect bliss
    Is the sunshine of ours.

<107>

If I could dwell
Where Israfel
  Hath dwelt, and he where I,
He might not sing so wildly well
  A mortal melody,
While a bolder note than this might swell
  From my lyre within the sky.

1831-1845

<108>

DREAMLAND

By a route obscure and lonely,
Haunted by ill angels only,
Where an Eidolon, named NIGHT,
On a black throne reigns upright,
I have reached these lands but newly
From an ultimate dim Thule —
From a wild weird clime that lieth, sublime,
Out of SPACE — out of TIME.

Bottomless vales and boundless floods,
And chasms, and caves, and Titan woods,
With forms that no man can discover
For the dews that drip all over;
Mountains toppling evermore
Into seas without a shore;
Seas that restlessly aspire,
Surging, unto skies of fire;
Lakes that endlessly outspread
Their lone waters — lone and dead —
Their still waters — still and chilly
With the snows of the lolling lily.

By the lakes that thus outspread
Their lone waters, lone and dead —
Their sad waters, sad and chilly
With the snows of the lolling lily —
By the mountains — near the river
Murmuring lowly, murmuring ever —
By the grey woods — by the swamp
Where the toad and the newt encamp —

<109>

By the dismal tarns and pools
  Where dwell the Ghouls —
By each spot the most unholy —
In each nook most melancholy, —
There the traveler meets aghast
Sheeted Memories of the Past —
Shrouded forms that start and sigh
As they pass the wanderer by —
White-robed forms of friends long given,
In agony, to the Earth — and Heaven.

For the heart whose woes are legion
'T is a peaceful, soothing region —
For the spirit that walks in shadow
'T is — oh, 't is an Eldorado!
But the traveler, traveling through it,
May not — dare not openly view it;
Never its mysteries are exposed
To the weak human eye unclosed;
So wills its King, who hath forbid
The uplifting of the fringèd lid;
And thus the sad Soul that here passes
Beholds it but through darkened glasses.

By a route obscure and lonely,
Haunted by ill angels only,
Where an Eidolon, named NIGHT,
On a black throne reigns upright,
I have wandered home but newly
From this ultimate dim Thule.

1844-1849

SONG

I bade thee stay. Too well I know
  The fault was mine — mine only:
I dared not think upon the past,
  All desolate and lonely.

I feared in memory's silent air
  Too sadly to regret thee —
Feared in the night of my despair
  I could not all forget thee.

Yet go — ah, go! those pleading eyes,
  Those low, sweet tones, appealing
From heart to heart — ah, dare I trust
  That passionate revealing?

For ah, those dark and pleading eyes
  Evoke too keen a sorrow —
A pang that will not pass away,
  With thy wild vows, tomorrow.

A love immortal and divine
  Within my heart is waking:
Its dream of anguish and despair
  It owns not but in breaking.

<111>

OUR ISLAND OF DREAMS

By the foam
Of perilous seas, in faery lands forlorn. — Keats

Tell him I lingered alone on the shore,
Where we parted, in sorrow, to meet never more;
The night wind blew cold on my desolate heart,
But colder those wild words of doom,
    "Ye must part?"

O'er the dark, heaving waters, I sent forth a cry;
Save the wail of those waters there came no reply.
I longed, like a bird, o'er the billows to flee,
From our lone island home and the moan of the sea:

Away — far away — from the wild ocean shore,
Where the waves ever murmur, "No more,
      never more;"

<112>

Where I wake, in the wild noon of midnight, to hear
That lone song of the surges, so mournful and drear.

When the clouds that now veil from us heaven's
      fair light,
Their soft, silver lining turn forth on the night;
When time shall the vapors of falsehood dispel,
He shall know if I loved him, but never how well.

         —Sarah Helen Whitman, 1849

<113>

ANNABEL LEE

It was many and many a year ago,
  In a kingdom by the sea,
That a maiden there lived
  whom you may know
  By the name of Annabel Lee;
And this maiden she lived with no other thought
  Than to love and be loved by me.

I was a child and *she* was a child,
  In this kingdom by the sea;
But we loved with a love that was more than love —
  I and my Annabel Lee —
With a love that the wingèd seraphs in Heaven
  Coveted her and me.

And this was the reason that, long ago,
  In this kingdom by the sea,
A wind blew out of a cloud by night,
  Chilling my Annabel Lee;
So that her highborn kinsmen came
  And bore her away from me,
To shut her up, in a sepulchre
  In this kingdom by the sea.

The angels, not half so happy in Heaven,
  Went envying her and me —
Yes! — that was the reason (as all men know,
  In this kingdom by the sea)
That the wind came out of the cloud,
  chilling And killing my Annabel Lee.

<114>

But our love it was stronger by far than the love
    Of those who were older than we —
    Of many far wiser than we —
And neither the angels in Heaven above,
    Nor the demons down under the sea,
Can ever dissever my soul from the soul
    Of the beautiful Annabel Lee: —

For the moon never beams without bringing
        me dreams
    Of the beautiful Annabel Lee;
And the stars never rise but I see the bright eyes
    Of the beautiful Annabel Lee: —
And so, all the night-tide, I lie down by the side
  Of my darling — my darling — my life
        and my bride,
In her sepulchre there by the sea,
  In her tomb by the sounding sea.

May-September 1849

<115>

WITHERED FLOWERS

Remembrances of happiness! to me
   Ye bring sweet thoughts
      of the year's purple prime,
Wild, mingling melodies of bird and bee,
   That pour on summer winds their silvery chime
Of balmy incense, burdening all the air,
   From flowers that by the sunny garden wall
Bloomed at your side, nursed into beauty there
   By dews and silent showers: but these to *all*
Ye bring. Oh! sweeter far than these the spell
   Shrined in those fairy urns for *me* alone;
For me a charm sleeps in each honeyed cell,
   Whose power can call back hours of rapture flown,
To the sad heart sweet memories restore,
Tones, looks, and words of love
      that may return no more.

<116>

THE LAST FLOWERS

The undying voice of that dead time,
With its interminable chime,
Rings on my spirit like a knell.[1]

Dost thou remember that Autumnal day
   When by the Seekonk's lonely wave we stood,
And marked the languor of repose that lay,
   Softer than sleep, on valley, wave and wood?

A trance of holy sadness seemed to lull
   The charmèd earth and circumambient air,
And the low murmur of the leaves seemed full
   Of a resigned and passionless despair.

Though the warm breath of summer lingered still
   In the lone paths where late her footsteps passed,
The pallid star-flowers on the purple hill
   Sighed dreamily, "We are the last! the last!"

---

[1] Poe. "Tamerlane," 22-24.

<117>

I stood beside thee, and a dream of heaven
    Around me like a golden halo fell!
Then the bright veil of fantasy was riven,
    And my lips murmured, "Fare thee well! —
        farewell!"

I dared not listen to thy words, nor turn
    To meet the mystic language of thine eyes,
I only felt their power, and in the urn
    Of memory, treasured their sweet rhapsodies.

We parted then, forever—and the hours
    Of that bright day were gathered to the past —
But, through long wintry nights, I heard the flowers
    Sigh dreamily, "We are the last! — the last!"

September 1849

<118>

THE CITY
IN THE SEA

Lo! Death has reared himself a throne
In a strange city lying alone
Far down within the dim West,
Where the good and the bad
   and the worst and the best
Have gone to their eternal rest.
There shrines and palaces and towers
(Time-eaten towers that tremble not!)
Resemble nothing that is ours.
Around, by lifting winds forgot,
Resignedly beneath the sky
The melancholy waters lie.

No rays from the holy heaven come down
On the long night-time of that town;
But light from out the lurid sea
Streams up the turrets silently —
Gleams up the pinnacles far and free —
Up domes — up spires — up kingly halls —
Up fanes — up Babylon-like walls —
Up shadowy long-forgotten bowers
Of sculptured ivy and stone flowers —
Up many and many a marvelous shrine
Whose wreathèd friezes intertwine
The viol, the violet, and the vine.

<119>

Resignedly beneath the sky
The melancholy waters lie.
So blend the turrets and shadows there
That all seem pendulous in air,
While from a proud tower in the town
Death looks gigantically down.
There open fanes and gaping graves
Yawn level with the luminous waves;
But not the riches there that lie
In each idol's diamond eye —
Not the gaily-jeweled dead
Tempt the waters from their bed;
For no ripples curl, alas!
Along that wilderness of glass —
No swellings tell that winds may be
Upon some far-off happier sea —
No heavings hint that winds have been
On seas less hideously serene.

But lo, a stir is in the air!
The wave — there is a movement there!
As if the towers had thrust aside,
In slightly sinking, the dull tide —
As if their tops had feebly given
A void within the filmy Heaven.
The waves have now a redder glow —
The hours are breathing faint and low —
And when, amid no earthly moans,
Down, down that town shall settle hence,
Hell, rising from a thousand thrones,
Shall do it reverence.

1831-1845

<120>

THE BELLS

I

Hear the sledges with the bells —
Silver bells!
What a world of merriment their melody foretells!
How they tinkle, tinkle, tinkle,
In the icy air of night!
While the stars that oversprinkle
All the Heavens, seem to twinkle
With a crystalline delight;
Keeping time, time, time,
In a sort of Runic rhyme,
To the tintinabulation that so musically wells
From the bells, bells, bells, bells,
Bells, bells, bells —
From the jingling and the tinkling of the bells.

<121>

II

Hear the mellow wedding bells,
Golden bells!
What,? a world of happiness their harmony foretells!
Through the balmy air of night
How they ring out their delight!
From the molten golden-notes
And all in tune
What a liquid ditty floats
To the turtle-dove that listens while she gloats
On the moon!
Oh, from out the sounding cells,
What a gush of euphony voluminously wells!
How it swells!
How it dwells
On the Future! how it tells
Of the rapture that impels
To the swinging and the ringing
Of the bells, bells, bells, bells,
Bells, bells, bells —
To the rhyming and the chiming of the bells!

<122>

III

Hear the loud alarum bells —
Brazen bells!
What a tale of terror, now, their turbulency tells!
In the startled ear of Night
How they scream out their affright!
Too much horrified to speak
They can only shriek, shriek,
Out of tune,
In a clamorous appealing to the mercy of the fire —
In a mad expostulation with the deaf and frantic fire,
Leaping higher, higher, higher,
With a desperate desire
And a resolute endeavor.
Now — now to sit, or never,
By the side of the pale-faced moon.
Oh, the bells, bells, bells!
What a tale their terror tells
Of despair!
How they clang, and clash, and roar!
What a horror they outpour
In the bosom of the palpitating air!
Yet the ear it fully knows,
By the twanging,
And the clanging,
How the danger ebbs and flows: —

<123>

Yet the ear distinctly tells,
In the jangling,
And the wrangling,
How the danger sinks and swells,
By the sinking or the swelling in the anger
of the bells —
Of the bells —
Of the bells, bells, bells, bells,
Bells, bells, bells —
In the clamor and the clangor of the bells!

<124>

IV

Hear the tolling of the bells —
Iron bells!
What a world of solemn thought their monody
compels!
In the silence of the night,
How we shiver with affright
At the melancholy meaning of the tone!
For every sound that floats
From the rust within their throats
Is a groan.
And the people — ah, the people —
They that dwell up in the steeple
All alone,
And who, tolling, tolling, tolling
In that muffled monotone,
Feel a glory in so rolling
On the human heart a stone —
They are neither man nor woman —
They are neither brute nor human —
They are Ghouls: —
And their king it is who tolls;
And he rolls, rolls, rolls, rolls
A Paean from the bells!
And his merry bosom swells
With the Paean of the bells!

<125>

And he dances and he yells;
Keeping time, time, time,
In a sort of Runic rhyme,
To the Paean of the bells —
Of the bells: —
Keeping time, time, time,
In a sort of Runic rhyme
To the throbbing of the bells —
Of the bells, bells, bells —
To the sobbing of the bells;
Keeping time, time, time,
As he knells, knells, knells,
In a happy Runic rhyme,
To the rolling of the bells —
Of the bells, bells, bells: —
To the tolling of the bells,
Of the bells, bells, bells, bells,
Bells, bells, bells —
To the moaning and the groaning of the bells.

July 1849

<127>

PROSERPINE, TO PLUTO, IN HADES

Nec repetita sequi curet Proserpina matrem[1]
—Virgil, *Georgics*, I. 39

I think on thee amid these spring-time flowers,
  On thee, my emperor, my sovran lord,
Dwelling alone in dim Tartarean towers
  Of thy dark realm, by earth and heaven abhorred,
Wandering afar by that Avernian river
Where dead kings walk and phantoms wail forever.

I think on thee in that stern palace regnant,
  Where no sweet voice of summer charms the air,
Where the vast solitude seems ever pregnant
  With some wild dream of untold despair.
Thy love, remembered, doth heaven's light eclipse;
I feel thy lingering kisses on my lips.

I languish for the late autumnal showers,
  The cool, cool plashing of the autumn rain,
The shimmering hoar-frost and fast-fading flowers,
  That give me back to thy dark realm again:
To thee I'll bring Sicilia's starry skies
  And all the heaven of summer in my eyes.

---

[1] *Nec repetita.* Virgil introduces the novel idea that Proserpina/Persephone refuses to answer her mother's call to return home.

<128>

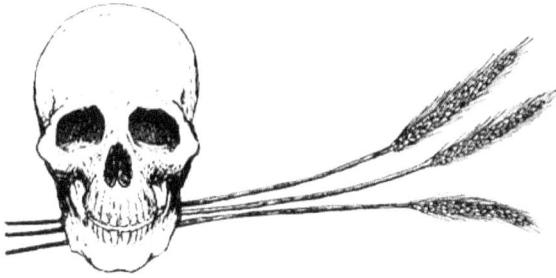

When from the earth's noontide beauty borne away
    To the pale prairies of that under world,
A mournful flower upon thy breast I lay
    Till round thy heart its clinging tendrils curled —
A frightened dove, that tamed its fluttering pinion
To the dear magic of thy love's dominion.

For thou wert grandly beautiful as night,
    Stern Orcus, in thy realm of buried kings;
And thy sad crown of cypress in my sight
    Fairer than all the bright and flowery rings
Of wreathèd poppies and of golden corn
By Ceres on her stately temples worn.

<129>

I sat beside thee on Hell's dusky throne,
  Nor feared the awful shadow of thy fate;
Content to share the burden of thy crown,
  And all the mournful splendors of thy state;
Bending my flower-like beauty to thy will,
Seeking with light thy lonely dark to fill.

Wondering, I think how thy dear love hath bound me
  In a new life that half forgets the old;
All day I haunt the meadows where you found me,
  Knee-deep in daffodils of dusky gold,
Or sit by Cyane's sad fountain, dreaming
Of the red lake by thy proud palace gleaming.

When, in her car by wingèd dragons borne,
  Pale Ceres sought me
    through the shuddering night,
With angry torches and fierce eyes, forlorn,
  Slaying the dark that screened me from her sight,
Like a reft lioness that rends the air
Of midnight with her perilous despair,

<130>

Jove, pitying the great passion of her woe,
    Gave back thy queen-bride to the mother's grief —
To Ceres gave — through summer's golden glow
    And all the crescent months, from spear to sheaf:
Alas, how sadly in Sicilian bowers
I pass this lonely, lingering time of flowers!

In the long silence of the languid noons,
    When all the panting birds are faint with heat,
I wander listless by the blue lagoons
    To hear their light waves rippling at my feet
Through the dead calm, and count the lingering time
By the slow pulsing of their silver chime.

I languish for the late autumnal showers,
    The cool, cool plashing of the autumn rain,
The shimmering hoar-frost and fast-fading flowers,
    That give me back to thy dark realm again;
I have no native land from thee apart,
And my high heaven of heavens is in thy heart.

<131>

THE CONQUEROR WORM

Lo! 't is a gala night
   Within the lonesome latter years!
An angel throng, bewinged, bedight
   In veils, and drowned in tears,
Sit in a theatre, to see
   A play of hopes and fears,
While the orchestra breathes fitfully
   The music of the spheres.

Mimes, in the form of God on high,
   Mutter and mumble low,
And hither and thither fly —
   Mere puppets they, who come and go
At bidding of vast formless things
   That shift the scenery to and fro,
Flapping from out their Condor wings
   Invisible Woe!

That motley drama — oh, be sure
   It shall not be forgot!
With its Phantom chased for evermore,
   By a crowd that seize it not,
Through a circle that ever returneth in
   To the self-same spot,
And much of Madness, and more of Sin,
   And Horror the soul of the plot.

<132>

But see, amid the mimic rout
    A crawling shape intrude!
A blood-red thing that writhes from out
    The scenic solitude!
It writhes! — it writhes! — with mortal pangs
    The mimes become its food,
And seraphs sob at vermin fangs
    In human gore imbued.

Out — out are the lights — out all!
    And, over each quivering form,
The curtain, a funeral pall,
    Comes down with the rush of a storm
While the angels, all pallid and wan,
    Uprising, unveiling, affirm
That the play is the tragedy, "Man,"
    And its hero the Conqueror Worm.

1842-1849

< 133 >

RESURGEMUS

I mourn thee not: no words can tell
  The solemn calm that
    tranced my breast
When I first knew thy soul had past
  From earth to its eternal rest;

For doubt and darkness, o'er thy head,
  Forever waved their Condor wings;
And in their murky shadows bred
  Forms of unutterable things;

And all around thy silent hearth,
  The glory that once blushed and bloomed
Was but a dim-remembered dream
  Of "the old time entombed."[1]

Those melancholy eyes that seemed
  To look beyond all time, or, turned
On eyes they loved, so softly beamed —
  How few their mystic language learned.
How few could read their depths, or know
  The proud, high heart that dwelt alone
In gorgeous palaces of woe,
  Like Eblis on his burning throne.

For ah! no human heart could brook
  That darkness of thy doom to share,
And not a living eye could look
  Unscathed upon thy dread despair.

---

[1] *Old time entombed*. From Poe's "Haunted Palace."

<134>

I mourn thee not: life had no lore
    Thy soul in morphean dews to steep,
Love's lost nepenthe to restore,
    Or bid the avenging sorrow sleep.

Yet, while the night of life shall last,
    While the slow stars above me roll,
In the heart's solitudes I keep
    A solemn vigil for thy soul.

I tread dim cloistral aisles, where all
    Beneath are solemn-sounding graves;
While o'er the oriel, like a pall,
    A dark, funereal shadow waves.

There, kneeling by a lampless shrine,
    Alone amid a place of tombs,
My erring spirit pleads for thine
    Till light along the orient blooms.

Oh, when thy faults are all forgiven,
    The vigil of my life outwrought
In some calm altitude of heaven —
    The dream of thy prophetic thought —

Forever near thee, soul in soul,
    Near thee forever, yet how far,
May our lives reach love's perfect goal
    In the high order of thy star!

<135>

SONNETS TO POE

I

Vainly my heart had with thy sorceries striven:
It had no refuge from thy love — no Heaven
But in thy fatal presence — from afar
It owned thy power and trembled like a star
O'erfraught with light and splendor. Could I deem
How dark a shadow should obscure its beam? —
Could I believe that pain could ever dwell
Where thy bright presence cast its blissful spell?
Thou wert my proud palladium — could I fear
The avenging Destinies when thou wert near? —
Thou wert my Destiny — thy song, thy fame,
The wild enchantments clustering round thy name,
Were my soul's heritage, its royal dower;
Its glory and its kingdom and its power!

II

When first I looked into thy glorious eyes,
  And saw, with their unearthly beauty pained,
Heaven deepening within heaven, like the skies
  Of autumn nights without a shadow stained,
I stood as one whom some strange dream enthralls;
  For far away, in some lost life divine,
Some land which every glorious dream recalls,
  A spirit looked on me with eyes like thine.
E'en now, though death has veiled their starry light,
And closed their lids in his relentless night —
As some strange dream, remembered in a dream,
Again I see, in sleep, their tender beam;
Unfading hopes their cloudless azure fill,
Heaven deepening within heaven, serene and still.

<136>

III

Oft since thine earthly eyes have closed on mine,
 Our souls, dim-wandering in the hall of dreams,
Hold mystic converse on the life divine,
 By the still music of immortal streams;
And oft thy spirit tells how souls, affied
 By sovran destinies, no more can part, —
How death and hell are powerless to divide
 Souls whose deep lives lie folded heart in heart.
And if, at times, some lingering shadow lies
 Heavy upon my path, some haunting dread,
Then do I point thee to the harmonies
 Of those calm heights whereto our souls arise
Through suffering, — the faith that doth approve
In death the deathless power and divine life of love.

IV

We met beneath September's gorgeous beams:
 Long in my house of life thy star had reigned;
Its mournful splendor trembled through my dreams,
 Nor with the night's phantasmal glories waned.
We wandered thoughtfully o'er golden meads
 To a lone woodland, lit by starry flowers,
Where a wild solitary pathway leads
  Through moldering sepulchres
   and cypress bowers.
A dreamy sadness filled the autumnal air —
 By a low, nameless grave I stood beside thee,
My heart according to thy murmured prayer
 The full sweet answers that my lips denied thee.
O mournful faith, on that dread altar sealed —
Sad dawn of love in realms of death revealed!

<137>

V

On our lone pathway bloomed no earthly hopes —
    Sorrow and death were near us, as we stood
Where the dim forest, from the upland slopes,
    Swept darkly to the sea. The enchanted wood
Thrilled, as by some foreboding terror stirred;
    And as the waves broke on the lonely shore,
In their low monotone, methought I heard
    A solemn voice that sighed, "Ye meet no more."
There, while the level sunbeams seemed to burn
    Through the long aisles of red, autumnal gloom—
Where stately, storied cenotaphs inurn
    Sweet human hopes, too fair on earth to bloom —
Was the bud reaped, whose petals, pure and cold,
Sleep on my heart till Heaven the flower unfold.

VI

If thy sad heart, pining for human love,
    In its earth solitude grew dark with fear,
Lest the high Sun of Heaven itself should prove
    Powerless to save from that phantasmal sphere
Wherein thy spirit wandered — if the flowers
    That pressed around thy feet, seemed
            but to bloom
In lone Gethsemanes, through starless hours,
    When all, who loved, had left thee to thy doom: —
Oh, yet, believe, that in that hollow vale,
    Where thy soul lingers, waiting to attain
So much of Heaven's sweet grace as shall avail
To lift its burden of remorseful pain —
My soul shall meet thee and its Heaven forego
Till God's great love, on both, one hope, one
        Heaven bestow.

<138>

ARCTURUS

Written in April
Nec morti esse locum, sed viva volare Sideris
in numerum atque alto succedere coelo
        —*VIRGIL,* Georgics, *IV*[1]

Again, imperial star! thy mystic beams
Pour their wild splendors on my waking dreams,
Piercing the blue depths of the vernal night
With opal shafts and flames of ruby light;
Filling the air with melodies, that come
Mournful and sweet, from the dark, sapphire dome —
Weird sounds, that make the cheek with wonder pale,
As their wild symphonies o'ersweep the gale,
For, in that gorgeous world, I fondly deem,
Dwells the freed soul of one whose earthly dream
Was full of beauty, majesty and woe;
One who, in that pure realm of thine, doth grow
Into a power serene — a solemn joy,
Undimmed by earthly sorrow or alloy;
Sphered far above the dread, phantasmal gloom —
The penal tortures of that living tomb
Wherein his earth-life languished — who shall tell
The drear enchantments of that Dantean hell!
"Was it not Fate, whose earthly name is Sorrow,"
That bade him, with prophetic soul, to borrow
From all the stars that fleck night's purple dome,
Thee, bright Arcturus! for his Eden home: —

---

[1] *For there is no place of annihilation: but alive they mount up each into his own
order of star, and take their high seat in the heavens*

<139>

Was it not Fate, whose name in Heaven above,
Is Truth and Goodness and unchanging Love —
Was it not Fate, that bade him turn to thee
As the bright regent of his destiny? —
For when thine orb passed from
      the lengthening gloom
Of autumn nights, a morning star to bloom
Beside Aurora's eastern gates of pearl,
He passed from earth, his weary wings to furl
In the cool vales of Heaven: thence, through yon sea
Of starry isles, to hold his course to thee.

Now, when in April's cloudless nights, I turn
To where thy pharos mid the stars doth burn —
A glorious cynosure — I read in thee
The rune of Virgil's golden augury;
And deem that o'er thy seas of silver calm
Floats the far perfume of the Eden palm.

<140>

THE PHANTOM VOICE

It is a phantom voice:
Again! — again! how solemnly it falls
Into my heart of hearts!"
— Scenes from Politian

Through the solemn hush of midnight,
    How sadly on my ear
Falls the echo of a harp whose tones
    I never more may hear!

A wild, unearthly melody,
    Whose monotone doth move
The saddest, sweetest cadences
    Of sorrow and of love:

Till the burden of remembrance weighs
    Like lead upon my heart,
And the shadow, on my soul that sleeps,
    Will never more depart.

The ghastly moonlight, gliding
    Like a phantom through the gloom,
How it fills with solemn fantasies
    My solitary room!

And the sighing winds of Autumn,
    Ah! how sadly they repeat
That low, bewildering melody,
    So mystically sweet!

<141>

I hear it softly murmuring
   At midnight o'er the hill,
Or across the wide savannas,
   When all beside is still.

I hear it in the moaning
   Of the melancholy main;
In the rushing of the night-wind,
   The rhythm of the rain.

E'en the wild flowers of the forest,
   Waving sadly to and fro,
But whisper to my boding heart
   The burden of its woe.

And the spectral moon, now paling
   And fading, seems to say,
"I leave thee to remembrances
   That will not pass away."

Ah, through all the solemn midnight,
   How mournful 't is to hark
To the voices of the silence,
   The whisper of the dark!

In vain I turn, some solace
   From the distant stars to crave:
They are shining on thy sepulchre,
   Are smiling on thy grave.

<142>

How I weary of their splendor!
   All night long they seem to say,
"We are lonely — sad and lonely —
   Far away — far, far away!"

Thus through all the solemn midnight,
   That phantom voice I hear,
As it echoes through the silence,
   When no earthly sound is near.

And though dawn-light yields to noon-light,
   And though darkness turns to day,
They but leave me to remembrances
   That will not pass away.

November 1849

<143>

TO ONE
IN PARADISE

Thou wast that all to me, love,
   For which my soul did pine —
A green isle in the sea, love,
   A fountain and a shrine,
All wreathed with fairy fruits and flowers,
   And all the flowers were mine.

Ah, dream too bright to last!
   Ah, starry Hope! that didst arise
But to be overcast!
   A voice from out the Future cries,
"On! On!" — but o'er the Past
   (Dim gulf!) my spirit hovering lies
Mute, motionless, aghast!

For, alas! alas! with me
   The light of Life is o'er!
"No more — no more — no more —"
(Such language holds the solemn sea
   To the sands upon the shore)
Shall bloom the thunder-blasted tree,
   Or the stricken eagle soar!

Alas! for that accursed time
   They bore thee o'er the billow
From Love — to titled age and crime,
   And an unholy pillow —
From me, and from our misty clime
   Where weeps the silver willow!

<144>

And all my days are trances,
　　And all my nightly dreams
Are where thy grey eye glances,
　　And where thy footstep gleams —
In what ethereal dances,
　　By what eternal streams.

1833

<145>

ALONE

From childhood's hour I have not been
As others were — I have not seen
As others saw — I could not bring
My passions from a common spring. —
From the same source I have not taken
My sorrow — I could not awaken
My heart to joy at the same tone —
And all I loved — *I* loved alone.
Then — in my childhood — in the dawn
Of a most stormy life — was drawn
From every depth of good and ill
The mystery which binds me still —
From the torrent, or the fountain —
From the red cliff of the mountain —
From the sun that round me rolled
In its autumn tint of gold —
From the lightning in the sky
As it pass'd me flying by —
From the thunder, and the storm—
And the cloud that took the form
(When the rest of Heaven was blue)
Of a demon in my view —

<146>

NOON

from "Hours of Life"

> *"The mysterious silence of full noon."*
> — BAILEY. *Festus.*

> *"Combien de fois dans le silence de minuit, et dans cet autre silence de midi, si accablant, si inquiet, si dévorant, n'ai-je pas senti mon coeur se précipiter vers un but inconnu, vers un bonheur sans forme et sans nom, qui est au ciel, qui est dans l'air, qui est partout, comme l'amour! C'est l'aspiration sainte de la partie la plus éthéreé de notre âme vers l'inconnu."*[1]
> — *George Sand*

Dream followed dream; and still the day
Floated on golden wings away;
But in the hush of the high noon,
Touched by a sorrow without name,
Consumed by a slow fever-flame,
I loathed my life's mysterious boon,
Unconscious of its end or aim;
Lost in a languor of repose —
    A luxury of gloom —
As when the curved, voluptuous rose
    Droops with its wealth of bloom.

Decked as for a festival
Seemed the wide and lonely hall
Of Nature, but a mute despair
Filled the universal air —
A sense of loneliness and void —

---

[1] How many times in the silence of midnight, and in the other silence of noon, whether overwhelming or anxious or raging, have I not felt my heart hurtling toward an unknown destination, toward a formless and nameless happiness, which is in the sky, in the air, everywhere, like love! It is the holy aspiration of the most etherial part of our soul toward the unknown.

<147>

A wealth of beauty unenjoyed —
A sadness born mid the excess
Of life's unvalued loveliness
Every pulse of being panting
With a bliss it fain would share,
Still there seemed a presence wanting,
Still some lost ideal haunting
All the lone and lustrous air.

Far off I heard the solemn chimes
    Of Life and Death —
The rhythm of ancestral rhymes
    Above — beneath!

"Light in shadow ever fading —
Death on Life's bright realm invading —
Pain with pleasure keeping measure,
Wasting care with golden treasure."
    So the ancient burden rang,
    So the choral verses sang.

Though beautiful on all the hills
The summer noon-light lay,
Far in the west a single cloud
Lay folded like a fleecy shroud,
Ready to veil its ray.
And over all a purple pall
Seemed waiting for the day.

I heard far, phantom voices calling
Over all the flowery wold —
O'er the westering meadows falling
Into slopes of gleamy gold —

<148>

Still I heard them calling — calling —
  Through the dim, entangled glooms —
Far through sunless valleys falling
  Downward to a place of tombs.

Near me pressed a vassal throng,
Slaves to custom, serfs to wrong —
Hollow-heart'd, vain and cold,
Minions of the earthly mold;
Holding in supreme derision
Memories of the life Elysian,
Reckless of the birthright lost,
Heedless of the heavenly host,
Traitors to the Holy Ghost!

Haunted by a nameless terror —
Thrilled by a foreboding breath,
As the aspen wildly trembles
When the winds are still as death —
I sought amid the sadness drear
Some loved familiar face to cheer
The solitude — some lingering tone
Of love ere love and hope had flown.

I heard a low voice breathe my name:
Was it the echo of my own —
That weird and melancholy tone—
That voice whose subtle sweetness came
Keen as the serpent's tongue of flame?
So near, its music seemed to me
The music of my heart to be.

<149>

Still I heard it, nearer, clearer,
When all other songs had flown,
Floating round me till it bound me
In a wild world of its own.

Suddenly a chill wind leapt
Through its woven harmonies —
All its silver chords were snapt
As a wind-harp's by the breeze.
A shudder through the silence crept
And death athwart the noon-light swept.

Then came the pall, the dirge, the knell,
As, dust to dust, the earth-clods fell,
Down crumbling on a coffin lid,
Within whose narrow casket hid —
Shut from the cheerful light of day —
Buried, yet quick, my own heart lay.

Graves closed round my path of life,
    The beautiful had fled;
Pale shadows wandered by my side,
    And whispered of the dead.
The far off hollow of the sky
    Seemed like an idle mockery —
The vaulted hollow of the sky,
    With its blue depths of mystery
    But rounded Death's vast empery.

<150>

O'erwearied with life's restless change
From ecstasy to agony,
Its fleeting pleasures born to die,
The mirage of its fantasy,
Its worn and melancholy range
Of hopes that could no more estrange
The married heart of memory,

Doomed, while we drain life's perfumed wine,
For the dull Lethean wave to pine,
And, for each thrill of joy, to know
Despair's slow pulse or sorrow's throe —
I sought some central truth to span
These wide extremes of good and ill —
I longed with one bold glance to scan
Life's perfect sphere, to rend at will
The gloom of Erebus — dread zone —
Coiled like a serpent round the throne
Of Heaven — the realm where Justice veils
Her heart and holds her even scales —
Where awful Nemesis awaits
The doomed, by Pluto's iron gates.

In the long noon-tide of my sorrow,
I questioned of the eternal morrow;
I gazed in sullen awe
Far through the illimitable gloom
Down deepening like the swift maelstrom,
The doubting soul to draw
Into eternal solitudes,
Where unrelenting silence broods
Around the throne of Law.

<151>

I questioned the dim chronicle
Of ages gone before —
I listened for the triumph songs
That range from shore to shore,
Where the heroes and the conquerors wrought
The mighty deeds of yore —
Where the footprints of the martyrs
Had bathed the earth in gore,
And the war-horns of the warriors
Were heard from shore to shore.

Their blood on desert plains was shed —
Their voices on the wind had fled —
They were the drear and shadowy DEAD!

Still, through the storied past, I sought
An answer to my sleepless thought;
In the cloisters old and hoary
Of the mediaeval time —
In the rude ancestral story
Of the ancient Runic rhyme.

I paused on Grecian plains, to trace
Some remnant of a mightier race,
Serene in sorrow and in strife,
Calm conquerors of Death and Life,
Types of the god-like forms that shone
Upon the sculptured Parthenon.

But still, as when Prometheus bare
From heaven the fiery dart,
I saw the "vulture passions" tear
The proud Caucasian heart —
The war of destiny with will
Still conquered, yet conflicting still.

<152>

I heard loud Hallelujahs
From Israel's golden lyre,
And I sought their great Jehovah
In the cloud and in the fire.
I lingered by the stream that flowed
"Fast by the oracle of God"[1] —
I bowed, its sacred wave to sip —
Its waters fled my thirsting lip.
The serpent trail was over all
Its borders — and its palms that threw
Aloft their waving coronal,
Were blistered by a poison dew.

Serener elements I sought,
Sublimer altitudes of thought,
The truth Saint John and Plato saw,
The mystic light, the inward law;
The Logos ever found and lost,
The aureola of the Ghost.

I hailed its faint auroral beam
In many a Poet's Delphic dream —
On many a shrine where faith's pure flame
Through fable's gorgeous oriel came.
Around the altars of the god,
In holy passion hushed, I trod,
Where one the mighty voice of Jove
Rang through Dodona's haunted grove.[2]
No more the dove with sable plumes
Swept through the forest's gorgeous glooms;
The shrines were desolate and cold,

[1] *Paradise Lost*, I, 12.

[2] "The priestesses of Dodona assert that two black pigeons flew from Thebes in Egypt; one of which settled in Libya, the other among themselves: which latter, resting on a beech tree, declared with a human voice that here was to be the oracle of Jove."—Herodotus, Book II, ch 55. — SHW

<153>

Their paeans hushed, their story told,
In long, inglorious silence lost,
Like fiery tongues of Pentecost.
No more did music's golden surge
The mortal in immortal merge:
High canticles of joy and praise
Died with the dream of other days;
I only heard the Maenad's wail —
That shriek that made the orient pale:
Evohe! — ah — evohe![1]
The mystic burden of a woe
Whose dark enigma none may know;
The primal curse — the primal throe.
Evohe! — ah — evohe!
Nature shuddered at the cry
Of that ancient agony!

Still the fabled Python bound me —
Still the serpent coil inwound me —
Still I heard the Maenad's cry,
Evohe! — ah — evohe!

---

[1] The Maenads, in their wild incantations, carried serpents in their hands, and with frantic gestures cried out Eva! Eva! Epiphanius thinks that this invocation related to the mother of mankind; but I am inclined to believe that it was the word *Epha* or *Opha*, rendered by the Greeks, *Ophis*, serpent. I take Abbadon to have been the name of the same ophite God whose worship has so long infected the world. The learned Heinsius makes Abbadon the same as the serpent Python."
—Jacob Bryant, *Analysis of Ancient Mythology*

"While Maenads cry *Evoe, Evoe!*
That voice that is contagion to the world."
— Shelley, *Prometheus Unbound*
—SHW

<154>

Where the Nile pours his sullen wave
Through tombs and empires of the grave,
I sought, 'mid cenotaphs, to find
The earlier miracles of mind:
Alas, beside the funeral urn
How drearily the death-lights burn;
On dim Denderah's sculptured lore
How sadly the noonlight falls,
How mournfully the west wind sighs
Through Karnak's moldering halls!
No tongue shall tell their wondrous tale,
No hand shall lift the Isis veil;

The mighty pyramids that rise
So drear along the morning skies,
Guard well the secrets of the dead,
Nor break the sleep of ages fled.

Their awful shadow passed, I stood
On India's burning solitude;
Where, in the misty morning of the world,
Life lay as in a dream of beauty furled.

I saw the mighty altars of the Sun —
Before whose fires, the star-gods, one by one,
Paled like thin ghosts — in lurid splendors rife;
I heard the Persian hail him Lord of Life!
I saw his altar flames rise wild and high,
Veiling the glory of the noon-day sky,
Hiding the holy heavens with their ensanguined dye.

<155>

I turned, and from the Brahmin's milder law
I sought truth's mystic element to draw,
Pure as it sparkled in the cup of Heaven —
The bright Amreeta to the immortals given —
To bathe my soul in fontal springs, that lie
Veiled from the careless and incurious eye.
Half wakened from the brooding sleep
Of Nature ere she felt the leap
Of sentient life, the Hindoo seemed
Sad as the faith his fathers dreamed;
Like his own rock-hewn temples, wrought
From some obscure and shadowy thought
Of ancient days —some formless dread,
In the gray dawn of ages bred —
Prone on his native earth reclined,
To endless reveries resigned,
His dull song lapsing on the Lethean stream,
Lost in the dim world of a lotus dream.

Still, still the eternal mystery
The shadow of the poison-tree
Of Good and Evil haunted me.
In Religion's holy name,
Furies fed her altar-flame,
Sophists gloried in her shame.
Still the ancient mythus bound me,
Still the serpent coil inwound me,
Still I heard the Maenad's cry,
Evohe! — ah — evohe!

<156>

Wearied with man's discordant creed,
I sought on Nature's page to read
Life's history, eye yet she shrined
Her essence in the incarnate mind;
Intent her secret laws to trace
In primal solitudes of space,
From her first, faint atomic throes,
To where her orbèd splendor glows
In the vast, silent spheres that roll
Forever towards their unknown goal.

I turned from dull alchemic lore
With starry Chaldeans to soar,
And sought, on fancy's wing, to roam
That glorious galaxy of light
Where mingling stars, like drifting foam,
Melt on the solemn shores of night;
But still the surging glory chased
The dark through night's chaotic waste;
And still, within its deepening voids,
Crumbled the burning asteroids.

Long gloating on that hollow gloom,
Methought that in some vast maelstrom
The stars were hurrying to their doom —
Bubbles upon life's boundless sea,
Swift meteors of eternity,
Pale sparks of mystic fire, that fall
From God's unwaning coronal.

<157>

Is there, I asked, a living woe
In all those burning orbs that glow
Through the blue ether? — do they share
Our dim world's anguish and despair?
In their vast orbits do they fly
From some avenging destiny —
And shall their wild eyes pale beneath
The dread anathema of Death?

Our own fair earth — shall she too drift,
Forever shrouded in a weft
Of stormy clouds, that surge and swirl
Around her in a dizzy whirl: —
Forever shall a shadow fall
Backward from her golden wall,
Its dark cone stretching, ghast and gray,
Into outer glooms away? —

From the sad, unsated quest
Of knowledge, how I longed to rest
On her green and silent breast!
I languished for the dews of death
    My fevered heart to steep —
The heavy, honey-dews of death,
    The calm and dreamless sleep.

<158>

I left my fruitless lore apart,
And leaned my ear on Nature's heart,
To hear, far from life's busy throng,
The chime of her sweet undersong.

She pressed her balmy lips to mine,
She bathed me in her sylvan springs;
And still, by many a rural shrine,
She taught me sweet and holy things.
I felt her breath my temples fan,
I learned her temperate laws to scan,
My soul, of hers, became a conscious part;
Her beauty melted through my inmost heart.

Still I languished for the word
Her sweet lips had never spoken,
Still, from the pale shadow-land,
There came nor voice nor token;
No accent of the Holy Ghost
Whispered of the loved and lost;
No bright wanderer came to tell
If, in worlds beyond the grave,
Life, love, and beauty dwell.

<159>

THE PORTRAIT

After long years I raised the folds
    concealing
That face, magnetic
    as the morning's beam
While slumbering memory thrilled at its revealing
    Like Memnon wakening from his marble dream.

Again I saw the brow's translucent pallor,
    The dark hair floating o'er it like a plume;
The sweet, imperious mouth, whose haughty valor
    Defied all portents of impending doom.

Eyes planet calm, with something in their vision
    That seemed not of earth's mortal mixture born;
Strange mythic faiths and fantasies Elysian,
    And far, sweet dreams of "fairy lands forlorn."[1]

Unfathomable eyes that held the sorrow
    Of vanished ages in their shadowy deeps,
Lit by that prescience of a heavenly morrow
    Which in high hearts the immortal spirit keeps.

Oft has that pale, poetic presence haunted
    My lonely musings at the twilight hour,
Transforming the dull earth-life it enchanted,
    With marvel and with mystery and with power.

Oft have I heard the sullen sea-wind moaning
    Its dirge-like requiems on the lonely shore,
Or listening to the Autumn winds intoning
    The wild, sweet legend of the lost Lenore;

---

[1] *Fairy lands forlorn.* From Keats' "Ode to a Nightingale."

<160>

Oft in some ashen evening of October,
    Have stood entranced beside a moldering tomb
Hard by that visionary lake of Auber,
    Where sleeps the shrouded form of Ulalume;

Oft in chill, star-lit nights have heard the chiming
    Of far-off mellow bells on the keen air,
And felt their molten-golden music timing
    To the heart's pulses, answering unaware.

Sweet, mournful eyes, long closed
      upon earth's sorrow
    Sleep restfully after life's fevered dream!
Sleep, wayward heart! till on some cool,
      bright morrow
    Thy soul, refreshed, shall bathe
      in morning's beam.

Though cloud and sorrow rest upon thy story,
    And rude hands lift the drapery of thy pall,
Time, as a birthright, shall restore the glory,
    And Heaven rekindle all the stars that fall.

1870

<161>

THE TOMB
OF EDGAR POE

Translated from Mallarmé

Even as Eternity his soul reclaimed,
The poet's song ascended in a strain
So pure, the astonished age that had defamed
Saw death transformed in that divine refrain.

While writhing coils of hydra-headed wrong,
Listening, and wondering at that heavenly song,
Deemed they had drank of some foul
    mixture brewed
In Circe's maddening cup, with sorcery inbued.

Alas! if from an alien to his clime,
No bas-relief may grace that font sublime,
Stern block, in some obscure disaster hurled
From the rent heart of a primeval world,

Through storied centuries thou shalt proudly stand
In the memorial city of his land,
A silent monitor, austere and gray,
To warn the clamorous brood of harpies
    from their prey.

1876

<162>

ABOUT THIS BOOK

The body type is Aldine, based on early typefaces created by Aldus Manutius, the great Venetian humanist printer and publisher. Headlines are set in Calligraph 421, a typeface inspired by hand-lettering.

The cover and book design is by Brett Rutherford, using art elements and illustrations by Richard Sardinha. Two of these illustrations incorporate the 1838 painting of Sarah Helen Whitman owned by the Providence Athenaeum and the 1848 daguerreotype of Edgar Allan Poe now housed at the John Hay Library at Brown University.

<163>

www.ingramcontent.com/pod-product-compliance
Lightning Source LLC
LaVergne TN
LVHW051348080426
835509LV00020BA/3334